A Living Classroom

Ideas for Student Creativity and Community Service

Ronald W. Poplau

ROWMAN & LITTLEFIELD
Lanham • Boulder • New York • London

Published by Rowman & Littlefield
An imprint of The Rowman & Littlefield Publishing Group, Inc.
4501 Forbes Boulevard, Suite 200, Lanham, Maryland 20706
www.rowman.com

6 Tinworth Street, London SE11 5AL, United Kingdom

British Library Cataloguing in Publication Information Available

Library of Congress Cataloging-in-Publication Data Available

ISBN 978-1-4758-4854-0 (pbk. : alk. paper)
ISBN 978-1-4758-4855-7 (electronic)

♾™ The paper used in this publication meets the minimum requirements of American National Standard for Information Sciences—Permanence of Paper for Printed Library Materials, ANSI/NISO Z39.48-1992.

Printed in the United States of America

*These pages are dedicated to the memory of my daughter,
Kristen Marie Poplau, the sunshine of my life.
Greatly missed and greatly loved.*

Contents

Foreword   ix

Preface   xi

1   Much to Do about Nothing: Anti-American Birds   1

2   You're a Son of a Gun: Let's Get down to Brass Tacks   5

3   Let's Find Out . . .   11

4   Student Creative Studies   15

5   Come on In: Guest Speakers   23

6   The Three Little Pigs   33

7   The Fox in the Henhouse   37

8   Color Blind   43

9   Perspectives on Death   51

10   Byron Andrew Grosko: July 30, 1965–March 29, 1983
Sean Joseph Grosko: February 11, 1969–May 7, 1985   59

11   Blue Skying   65

12   A Community Service Class: The Philosophical Basis   71

13   The Mechanics of a Community Service Class   75

14 A Case Study: Heather   81

15 Bells and Cells   85

16 From Russia with Questions   91

Appendix A: Community Comments   95

Appendix B: Awards   97

Appendix C: Tests and Methods   99

Appendix D: Forms   105

References   115

About the Author   117

Foreword

"Life Begins When You Get out of Your Comfort Zone!"

Ron Poplau, legendary social studies teacher at Shawnee Mission Northwest High School, gave opportunity after opportunity to his students to experience life-changing events by taking them out of their comfort zone. Each semester he brought in seventy guest speakers who shared stories and ideas his classes would never have heard, and I was one of them. I was also involved when he brought men who were incarcerated at the Lansing Correctional Facility to interact with his students. The men were members of Reaching Out From Within and their sole purpose was to become completely "raw, real, and relevant" to the extent that no student in that classroom would ever enter a prison.

Many of the students were dealing with delinquency issues and were on probation.

Ron challenged his students to relinquish mindsets that were closed to new possibilities. He kept pushing their envelopes and even his own. He shifted into arranging for them to engage in community service. His initial class on community service became so popular that he had to offer two classes, and then a whole day of classes and there were still waiting lists of students who wanted to be part of this unique, creative classroom learning experience.

Ultimately, he gave up teaching social studies and designed an array of amazing community service activities that captured the hearts and minds of thousands of students. He empowered them to change their attitudes about the elderly, to change their behaviors with students who had disabilities, to create their own activities that took them way beyond the scope of taking tests, and dealing with adolescent angst.

Ron was a genius at bringing the outside world into the classroom and taking the classroom into the outside world. One of my favorite stories about his community service vision was when he took students to visit senior citizens in retirement homes. What began as a charming project turned into a formal "prom" with tuxedos, corsages, dancing partners, and an indelible memory. Ron was recognized at the state and national level as "Teacher of the Year." Decades later you can speak with any graduate of Shawnee Mission Northwest High School and they may not remember the name of their algebra instructor or their history teacher, but every alum would speak reverently about the celebrated Ron Poplau.

Many of his students went on to become community leaders and activists and/or chose careers in the helping professions. His imprint extended into changing the culture of the school and ultimately the culture of the community at large. Once you connected with his enthusiasm, his creativity, and his energy, you shared his belief that when you give, you receive—immeasurably. Can you just imagine if "community service" was a required class in *every* high school in America? Can you just imagine the impact on our national value system? Can you just imagine our country bonded by a shared appreciation for the human spirit? The purpose of life is to find a purpose in your life. Ron Poplau knows that in the core of his being, and his book will inspire the transformational gift of community service across our land.

"Our education system is devoted to bringing knowledge to students—Ron Poplau brings them wisdom."

SuEllen Fried
Writer, bullying prevention activist, educator
Board Member: Bully Safe USA

Life member: Prevent Child Abuse America
President emeritus: Reaching out from Within
Advisory board: Friends of Alvin Ailey
Member: Authors Guild
Charter Member: American Dance Therapy Association

Preface

Stop! Please do not put this unique book back on the shelf until you have read this entire preface. Why? Contained in these pages are more than fifty years of teaching in almost every environment. I consider this a form of legacy. According to the statistical average, I am past the possibility of writing another book. I simply want to share. My teaching experiences span every venue: from elementary to the college level. I now ask myself: what was effective? To be honest, I wrote this book with myself in mind. I dislike long books with excess verbiage. I really am not concerned with what I am doing, but what is being done.

Consider this like an overture to an opera. It will become obvious that I am a staunch opponent of "read and recite, tell and test, sit and get!" Those approaches are an outrage! They are contrary to the true nature of education. What are the alternatives? Is status quo the best we can do?

Chapters are short. You can read an entire one in a single setting. You will very quickly find that I am the foremost advocate of community service and student creativity. However, the community service I advocate should be part of the daily school curriculum. For the past twenty-six years, students in my high school, Shawnee Mission Northwest, have devoted at least one whole class period a day, five days a week to community service.

Why is this approach so important rather than an adjunct to the school day? A future chapter will spell this out and also offer a "how to." In this age of technological miracles, "high tech" must be matched with "high touch." Even before the advent of the Internet, Marshall McLuhan firmly believed that when today's students come to school, in effect they interrupt their education! In all too many instances, I tend to agree with him.

In addition to daily community service, creativity is near the top of the educational process at every level. I especially urge you to read chapter one.

Through creativity, Ewen Montagu personally masterminds the greatest act of deception in the whole history of warfare. His type sits in every classroom. In a way, students can produce their own "curriculum" with only a green light from their instructors.

Experience is the best teacher. We all know that. Now more than ever we must make that a reality. In future chapters you will find examples of how students produced their own dynamic examples of personal creativity. There are exercises to "wake up" the latent creativity of those enrolled in our classes. Do these exercises work? Yes!

There is a basic unity to these many diverse chapters. All of us have heard that "one size does not fit all." I adamantly content that it is "two sizes" that fit all: creativity and community service. We should never put new wine in old flakes! Creativity comes from within. When students take charge of their learning—they learn!

Community service performed on a daily basis sparks a latent flame that transforms the very nature of "the doer of good becomes good." Heather's story is a living proof of the transformable effect of serving others. She was near death when she entered my classroom. Her mother dreaded every phone call expecting her daughter's demise. Like the Phoenix she became an adult, caring spirit.

A glance at the table of contents indicates the major concerns of education today. Charles Reich in The Greening of America held that "nothing is nailed down, everything is coming up." While we are in this state of flux, let's overhaul the whole system of education in America. Teachers need to take control of their profession. Remove it once and for all from all special interest groups. We need to return to the very basics of education itself. Guided by the philosophy "Students Are Number One," Shawnee Mission Northwest gained both a national and international reputation.

These are not new ideas but a resurrection of the soul of teaching:

1. Creativity
2. Community service
3. Origins of culture
4. Perspectives on death
5. The future
6. Prisons

Our district in a relatively short period of time changed to over thirty percent minority. Adjustment for the diverse cultures took much creativity. Death is a major part of each of our lives. It should not be comparable to a "plane shot out of the sky." On the average, all our lives consist of 30,000 days. We can equip our students with the skills and qualities to make them "a life well lived."

Unfortunately, all too many of our students populate our many and growing number of prisons. One middle school instructor, my daughter, had nine students incarcerated for crimes including murder. Everyone in prison was once one of our students. Our commitment to their well-being does not end with their graduation. Ninety percent will someday return to our communities. Has the prison rehabilitated or simply punished them.

I experienced the environment of a major prison when I did counseling work there for eleven years. An inmate was stabbed to death in my presence! Several inmates were from my school district. Their appearance changed almost overnight.

It was my experience that community service not only changed the character of students, but myself as well. My intention is not self-gratification by any means. I do not stand in my student's spotlights but in their halos! On the final day of the semester, it resembles sending my own children off to college. In tears we mutually bid farewells determined to make something out of their lives by helping others. Heather's mother said it best, "This was a class from God!" I share that divine sentiment. I simply want to pass it on.

Chapter 1

Much to Do about Nothing

Anti-American Birds

Creativity is a highly effective skill. Plato's system of epistemology would have us believe that it is embedded in every person. The secret is to find the proper stimulus to actualize it. The World War II story of Major William Martin has long been considered the most successful and creative deception in the history of warfare. The genius of Ewen Martin saved countless allied lives. The complete details of this deception project are still held in confidence by the British.

We are uncertain of the real name of William Martin. What was the "stimulus" that released this creative project? What was his educational background? Likewise, how do ordinary doves become anti-American in the Korean War? Is it possible for today's teachers to duplicate or embed the skill of creativity? Both of these examples—and there are many more—are a tribute to the British teachers and others professionals! These skills cannot be achieved by "read and recite, tell and test" or "sit and get!"

Wars are not won by the most powerful country
But by the country that makes the least mistakes.

Dawn is breaking over Huelva, Spain. It is April 1943. The sky is overcast. A light breeze produces a sea of waves parallel to the shore. Suddenly with the aid of binoculars an object can be seen drifting to the shore. It appears to be a body. Immediately a boat races to the floating corpse. Around its neck is a Mae West (a flotation collar). The body appears to be of a British pilot. No doubt his plane has crashed on the way to possibly Algiers. There is a mysterious briefcase chained to his wrist.

Examination of the body produced his military identity as William Martin. His trench coat was filled with such common personal things as pencil stubs,

1

cash, receipts, bus tickets, cigarettes, keys, and even an engagement ring. The body was delivered to the local police who had ties with the Germans.

The briefcase contained the most useful and precious information. It was nothing short of a treasure trove "of vital war-time information." It contained two letters—one signed by Sir Archibald Nye and the other by none other than Lord Mountbatten. The strategic information indicated that the imminent invasion would be of Greece, not Sicily as everyone expected. Churchill was convinced that it was only logical to invade by way of Sicily. The secret from the briefcase indicated the surprise attack would be on Greece with only a mere cover attack on Sicily.

This new information would be immediately transmitted to the German command in Berlin. On May 4, the Fuhrer acted quickly. Based on that "secret information" obtained in the briefcase, he sent the First Panzer Division halfway across Europe. He would thwart the Greece attack with military might that included guns, mines, and torpedo boats. So convinced was he of the "secret" information from that briefcase, thirteen days after the allied landings in Sicily, the Fuhrer thought it was merely the cover attack.

Meanwhile, in the cemetery at Huelva, the solemn faced British brought this episode to a close by placing a wreath on the grave of William Martin. The casualty list in the British newspaper carried the news of the loss of William Martin. The fake fiancé produced the needed tears for the loss of her future husband.

Let's process the above lengthy, macabre, and perverse story. William Martin never existed—"he never was." The entire episode was the brain child of Ewen Montagu. He searched London for the "right" body: someone who had died from a disease that filled his lungs with fluid. He would then resemble a person who had drowned at sea. He put the body in cold storage. He asked himself, "What would a military authority carry on his person that would in the final analysis simulate normalcy?"

Not only was he donned in a military uniform, but parts of his body needed to be thawed out to accommodate his new identity. The "fake" letters were placed in the briefcase together with lengthy pages of book proofs of history and the illustrations of history of British commanders. These items were the justification of the use of the briefcase.

The end result of this ingenious plan was the saving of thousands of allied lives. Even a Hollywood movie starring Clifton Webb, glorified the creativity of Ewen Montagu. The final file on this was never released until Margaret Thatcher consented to release it in 1984! Montagu never fully realized the ultimate effect of his creation. Only days before he died did he learn the complete details of his famous deception.

You must be asking, "What on earth is the significance of this story and why is it part of a book on education?" Obviously, Ewen Montagu had to think outside the box. There was no precedent for this project. It was entirely up to his creative ability. Most of us have heard about *The Trojan Horse* example of centuries ago. Most historians now consider that to be nothing but a myth—a made up story. There wasn't even a hint of "read and recite, tell and test" in the William Martin project. Historians all agreed it was the greatest act of deception in all of history. Ewen did not sit in a British classroom characterized by "sit and get."

He had attended the British school of Westminster in London which specialized in the creative approach to learning. The important question for educators is how to unlock the innate or latent creativity in all our students? We do not need more INFORMATION but more FORMATION. All this is merely the tip of the iceberg. With the explosion of knowledge no one has the ability to retain even a small percentage of it. We know that all behavior is learned behavior.

Skills must be the uppermost objective in our lesson plans. Ask yourself, "How many of our students could produce a 'William Martin'?" Our students must look at something that many so-called authorities have looked at and see something new or different. Montagu had to convince the enemy that what they found was real!

To intentionally digress for a moment, what makes a symphonic conductor different? What made Toscanini, Ormandy, Dorati, and Solti such great conductors? Each had the identical score, and sometimes the identical orchestra, for example, Beethoven's Fifth Symphony. Their final "versions" were unique. Compare the opening notes of that symphony conducted by Leonard Bernstein, then by Bruno Walter. Each saw something different or created something new and unique.

Do we need another Montagu today? The newsprint is filled with accusations of "fake" news, subliminal messages, and so on. Within limits, the teacher can liberate the creative skills within each student.

"William Martin" is on our attendance rosters. He waits in an endless sea for an outlet of creativity. Future chapters of this book give examples of "how to" unlock the personal skills in all of us. Think about the contributions of Jonas Salk and others. Who were their teachers? Think of all the current problems such as the "green island," that cry out for innovative solutions.

If you are a first grade teacher, YOU will be the only first grade teacher that child will ever have! The same can be said for every grade and every subject. Too often many teachers teach from a script, the student memorizes lines and facts as if they are part of a play. Ewen Montagu will be forever remembered for producing someone who "never was." Teachers daily deal with "someone who is!" Read on about another interesting example of creativity to influence the enemy.

This time the place is Pyongyang, Korea. Well might we ask, how is it possible to train birds—doves—to be anti-American?—operative conditioning. This involves no floating corpse loaded with fake information to confuse the enemy. As of this writing, there is no conclusion to the Korean War, only an armistice. Consequently, a United Nations delegation meets regularly in a neutral building in Pyongyang. This is how some North Korean officials turned the dove, the universal symbol of peace, to be anti-American with creative success.

North Korean operatives flew over the peace compound taking a long, detailed photograph of the entire compound. In this manner, they got a "bird's-eye view" of all the major buildings. The next step was to construct a huge complex as it would be seen from the dove's perception. They enclosed the complex in a large screened cage. The allied and communist buildings were clearly visible. Each allied building was given an electric charge. It was not sufficient to kill the doves but strong enough to make each landing uncomfortable.

After several weeks of this conditioning, the doves avoided any allied buildings. When the United Nations delegation arrived, the doves were released. To a bird, they only landed on the communist buildings. The communists were eager to point out that even the doves were on their side. The impression was "obvious." Was it effective? As of this writing, no peace treaty has concluded that war which ended in 1953. Again, wars are not won by the more powerful country, but by the country that makes the least mistakes. Score another victory for creativity.

The list of creativity marches on. Planes were "painted" on runways to confuse enemy pilots; inflatable rubber tanks to give the impression of a well-fortified area; Dutch pilots were given huge lists of fake information and then dropped behind enemy lines. Knowing in advance that they would be captured and subjected to truth serum, they were instructed to take cyanide tablets rather than divulge military secrets. Problem: the cyanide tablets were fake. The enemy was under the "impression" that the information they received was correct and planned accordingly. (Eventually all the Dutch pilots were liberated!).

Go to your computers and look up Clifton James or better yet, read his book. He was an actor who doubled for General Montgomery to mislead the Germans. "Monty" was so effective, he even fooled Montgomery's own staff. The list could almost be endless. The point is simply the power and effect of creativity. Teachers cannot use the *jeopardy* approach to education: giving the students five seconds to respond with the correct answer. What skills will your students develop as a result of your teaching? Nothing is more powerful than an idea that has come into its own!!!

Chapter 2

You're a Son of a Gun

Let's Get down to Brass Tacks

The mind is not a vessel to be filled, but a fire to be kindled.

—Plutarch

The beginning of creativity begins with the word, why. In place of a sponge activity at the beginning of each class, try one of these expressions. Their meaning and others can be found with the assistance of a computer. Ask students to suggest other expressions that seem puzzling to them. Reserve a few minutes for the class to write some expressions. Why do we ask, "Did you get up on the wrong side of the bed this morning? Is there a correct side?"

Brand names of everyday products are extremely interesting: Noxzema, Quaker Oats. Quakers have tried for years to have their name removed from the product. By the way, why is the Society of Friends called Quakers? The list can be almost endless!

Related to the origin of expressions is the existence of the subliminal. Things are not always what they appear to be. Two excellent sources that explain this phenomenon are *Subliminal Seduction* and *Media Sexploitation*. Both written and illustrated by Wilson Bryan Key. According to Key, the advertising message is actually on the back side of the article we are reading. The advertisement "bleeds through."

Students love this kind of observation. Motion pictures are loaded with subliminal messages. Students begin to question and analyze what they have always just taken for granted. Many popular stores have music in the background for shoppers to enjoy. Embedded in a great deal of the music is the admonition, "Pay for what you pick up?" Is it effective? Why is it when we shop for one or two items, we end up with a cart full or products? Impulsive

5

buying or is it "suggestive buying?" Expressions and the subliminal create an inquisitive mind!

The author transferred the numerous illustrations from Key's books to slides for more effective viewing by the class. To accomplish this, the binding of the paperbacks became undone. Without any request or prompting, students replaced both "damaged" books. Why? So future students would have access to them. In addition to replacement, students brought several of their friends to see the subliminal illustrations.

They found the chapter on *The Exorcist* especially of interest and value. This gave them perception skills for numerous advertisements and other motion pictures. These books gave them skills which they began applying outside of the classroom. Often they would bring pictures they began to see challenged their ability to analyze. How refreshing to experience this growth!

"There goes anyone who believes in nobody called everybody so they won't have to be somebody!" "The best way to get along, is to go along." How true those two ideas are of today's society. We give lip service to "think for yourself." "Be your own person." Ask yourself, do we live in a society that rewards individual thinking? What is the ultimate objective, the expectation in our classrooms? Everybody? Somebody?

A principal related this true example of one of his classrooms. The classroom of students was by far the most incorrigible in his entire building. The first teacher he hired lasted only two days. He abruptly quit saying, "Those students are beyond control!" The second teacher lasted a total of three days with the same conclusion. Even the principal believed that group was beyond the reach of any teacher. A third teacher was introduced to that unruly group of students.

All was quiet on the very first day! On the second day he observed a very organized classroom. Several days later, expecting the teacher to quit, he calmly asked the novice teacher what his secret was. No prior teacher achieved what he done. Somewhat baffled the teacher simply remarked that the class in question was gifted. "See," he said, showing the principal the attendance roster. "Their IQs are listed behind their names." Amazed, the principal remarked that those were not their IQs but their locker numbers!

Students will rise to the level of our expectations. Ask yourself, what kind of a student do you want? All is well that begins well. Many teachers use a sponge activity, that is, something written on the board, for example, a math problem to be solved or a paragraph to be read in the text book. However, we want students to think not just be good researchers. How can we do this?

Rene Descartes long ago gave us the expression, "Cogito ergo sum" which we translate, "I think, therefore I am." Well might we reverse this phrase and say, "I am, therefore I think!" Let's see how this works.

"Good morning class. I have a problem with which you can help me? What is the abbreviation for number?" It doesn't take long before a student will give the answer: no. "Thank you, you are right but there is no O in number." Where does that suddenly come from? This is different—much different—from a usual sponge activity. Students begin to try to find some reasonable answer. After some discussion, you give them the correct answer: the original word for number was numero. Now comes a brief discussion of a carryover from numerology or some form of epistemology.

What follows are a variety of expressions. Each has its own original meaning. Culture is a way of life with supporting ideas. We have forgotten the ideas but retain the expression. Here are a list of expressions that will cause students to think creatively. The answers can be found by the use of your computer.

"What is the origin of the expression?" There are many books that give us the original meaning. Rudolph Brash has several just waiting for your use. Try these:

1. Why do we tug at the wishbone of a turkey? Even at a formal dinner. Where is this practice alluded to in sacred scripture?
2. What is the meaning of "let's get down to brass tacks?"
3. Why is someone called a "son of a gun?" Guns do not have children.
4. Why is a baker's dozen 13?
5. Why do we tie cans on the bumper of a newly married couple?
6. Why do we give a twenty-one-gun salute to the president and only seven to a lesser official?
7. Were a number of black birds really baked in a pie?
8. What are the dog days of summer? Dogs live through all the other seasons?
9. This car will stop on a dime?
10. I'm on cloud nine—what are the other eight?
11. Why is coffee called a "cup of Joe?" We have a TV news program called *Morning Joe*.
12. What is the origin of the Christmas tree? Why cut down a perfectly good tree for about three weeks of display and covered with many lights and ornaments?
13. What is the origin of the honeymoon? A moon is not made of honey so why the reference?
14. By the skin of your teeth—teeth do not have skin!
15. Where did the word "Oscar" come from for movie awards?
16. Here's a good one: Why is Rhode Island called an island? It is far from being an island.
17. How is someone "upstaged?"

18. Speak up, "cat got your tongue?"
19. Why is it called a monkey wrench? It doesn't even resemble a monkey.
20. Why is alcohol called booze?
21. Why do we have Easter eggs and why are they colored. Rabbits don't lay eggs. Scripture and tradition gives us a hint as to their origin and color.
22. Why do we say "on the wagon?" How did drinking influence a wagon?
23. What is Tonto saying to the Lone Ranger: *Kemosabe*? While we are at it, what does Tonto mean?
24. Why do storks deliver babies?
25. It is raining cats and dogs? Brazilians say it is raining jack knives. Any connection?
26. What is the origin of pink for girls, blue for boys?
27. Why is an actor referred to as a "movie star?"
28. What is the origin of the military salute? (hint: medieval knights)
29. Life is a bowl of cherries. Why?
30. Why does the bride wear a veil?
31. Why do cats have nine lives?
32. Why a wreath: Christmas, funerals, other holiday wreaths. Why do we throw rice at a bride? What has this got to do with babies?
33. Three sheets in the wind?
34. Check out the origin of brand names—why do we say it is brand new?
35. You're fired! We now know it means you are terminated. The origin of this expression is one of the most interesting expressions. Look it up, it is worth the search.

All of these expressions and more can be easily found by the use of the computer. Just key in "What is the origin?" You will soon find that you will be unable to start a class unless you challenge them with an expression. Soon—very soon—students will ask you the origin of some expression that now begins to bother them. Put an "in put" box in the room. You will find it will quickly fill up.

Once the students' minds are activated, they won't rest until they get answers.

The teacher will enjoy the facial expressions of satisfaction as they discover origins of phrases. This is merely the beginning. Read on how students began to think of creative ways to either test or learn how people act and perhaps why.

Rudolph Brasch made it his life's work to research expressions. His book, "*How Did It Begin*," is excellent as well as "*How Did Sex Begin*," which is the origin of expressions relating to marriage. A short paperback book by Jeff Rovin, "*Why Do Cowboys Wear High Heels*" is also an excellent resource book on expressions. Rovin is the author of more than eighty books!

What effect do all these expressions have on student creativity? They begin to question why.

One teacher assigned each student to find the origin of phrases. Ashley Montagu researched swear words in almost every culture. Why do we invent words, gestures, phrases that have only one purpose: to insult. Even the Aborigines delighted in some very choice swear words.

Now let's look at how students have applied this creative exercise. Remember the success of the deception of William Martin in 1943. These students have outdone themselves with "new knowledge." During class reunions, they always ask, "Do you remember my original study?"

The teacher's response is simply, "Do you? It has been nearly fifty years!" Many sign their letters, "without wax." This is the original meaning of "sincerely."

DISCUSSION

As you well know, there are numerous other phrases that have an interesting origin. "You're fired" is especially interesting. Some have suggested it may have originated from the verb, "to discharge a gun." A more interesting origin and possibly more plausible one came from the odd behavior of John Henry Patterson. He would actually weigh his employees every six months. He disagreed with one of his employees at the National Cash Register Company, Thomas Watson Sr. He sent him away on a business deal. While Watson was gone, Watson's desk was thrown out on the lawn and set on fire, hence the phrase "you are fired."

Most of us say "One for the money, two for the show, three to get ready, and four to go!" This phrase refers to horse racing. Most of us do not "horse race" but have adopted that phrase as an expression with an entirely different meaning!

Choose some incident that most people might know and create an expression. Words that come to my mind are "Titanic," "Columbine," "Helter Skelter," and "Charles Manson." Often, we just use initials in place of a name, FDR, LBJ, JFK, MLK, CCC, and so on. Have the students come up with an expression that most people would understand NOW but later its true meaning might either be lost or changed. We use brand names like Scotch Tape, Kleenex, Xerox, but they in fact refer to some other manufacturer.

Check out the origin of booze or simply any popular brand. Did you know that in 2004, Donald J. Trump actually filed a trademark application for the catch phrase, "you're fired?"

Teaching is much more than imparting knowledge. The greatest minds in world history were not filled with knowledge alone. The academic records (report cards) of Edison, Einstein, were at best, average or below. They excelled in original thinking. The author agrees with Haim Ginott who references this poignant message from a principal to his staff at the beginning of a school year:

> I am a survivor of a concentration camp. My eyes saw what no man should witness: gas chambers built by learned engineers. Infants killed by trained nurses. Women and babies shot and burned by high school and college graduates. So, I am suspicious of education. Help your students become human. Your efforts must never produce learned monsters, skilled psychopaths or educated Eichmann's. Our minds are like parachutes, they only function when they are open! The mind in any race is a terrible thing to waste. The author's favorite college professor said, "A good teacher raises more questions than students can answer." So effective was he, that he began every class admonishing the author to limit himself to just one question! Open minds and community service will never and can never, produce an Eichmann. We all say rather flippantly, "A penny for your thoughts." That is far too cheap!

Chapter 3

Let's Find Out . . .

The man who has no imagination, has no wings.

—Muhammad Ali

Students are assigned to discover some information that is not currently available. After explaining the ten types of studies, students have two weeks to personally discover something new. A list of the ten different types of studies can be found in this book's appendix. Many students zero in on number nine: the participant/observer type. The only assistance from the instructor is a simple green light and verifying that nothing illegal is planned. One student enlisted the assistance of the vice-principal. The vice-principal actually interrupted a freshman class and also a senior class to break the news that the United States was under attack from Iran.

Only the classroom teacher in each instance was aware that this was an original study. The actual announcement can be found in the appendix. The comparative results were the exact opposite. Check the appendix to see how freshman and seniors responded. Students were proud of their original work and eager to share their conclusions with others. Sociologists list ten different kinds of original studies available for research. A complete listing can be found in the final chapter of this book.

Any standard sociology textbook will explain them in detail. Each of these studies is designed to produce sociological truth. By definition, mathematics is the only exact science. It is simply abstract reasoning. The sum of five and five will always be a predicable ten. However, it ceases to be exact when we ascribe it to something tangible, for example, five trees and five trees because each tree is a difference size. The final conclusion of these studies is what is true of the group average.

Human activity is always changing. Compare a photograph of yourself taken ten years ago with your current one.

It was the Greek philosopher, Heraclites, who held that the only constant was change. His most famous remark was, "Man cannot step into the same water twice, it flows on."

Emile Durkheim did the first sociological study "The Nature and Causes for Suicide." Some of his conclusions are no longer valid—they have flowed on. Today's computers have changed much of his studies.

Human nature is the same the world over. Humans everywhere possess freedom to choose. They are, however, affected by external stimuli such as color, sound and almost an endless array of vital forces. Are there some attributes that divide humans into groups? It is this group phenomenon that sociologists study to arrive at a conclusion. Many groups of serial killers have three things in common:

1. Animal cruelty
2. Pyromaniacs
3. Bed wetting

Not every one of the above is a serial killer. These traits are the result of what is called "the sociological average." "William Martin" was both a planned study that developed into a case study. The outcome was predicated depending on multiple actions. It was a gamble. Montagu had it all planned out. In this case, "all's well that ends well."

Confronted by the choice of ten "ways to go," students are on their own to choose and execute a study that will produce some new and original knowledge. No one is ever assigned a topic. The only assistance the instructor gives is procedural. However, some topics are either illegal or need special permission. One student's study produced a man hunt for the instructor. Involved were the district attorney, FBI, postal inspectors, plus the local police.

The student simply did not file the necessary procedural forms. However, it was an authoritative and a well-executed study. Ironically, the DA was so impressed with the cleverness and quality of the student's study, that he and the instructor became and remain best friends. The controversial study is included in this chapter.

The subjects that challenge students included such topics as

1. Honesty in public
2. Gay marriage
3. Gullibility
4. Use of the subliminal
5. Perception of a felony
6. Racism
7. Roles for men and women
8. Fake protestor
9. Christmas card study
10. Fake PA announcement

Students were cautioned not to do anything illegal or against district policy. When in doubt, always check with the teacher. For the sake of objectivity, students could not use school time. They were not permitted to employ the services of other sociology students except as confederates. They were given two weeks to complete their studies. Each study was then explained to the class by its author. What happened was both unexpected and nothing short of amazing.

Ewen Montagu would have been pleased. In some instances, it was similar to the man who never was. Read on for the results. Some of their studies were printed in national publications. When students return even fifty years later, they proudly ask, "Do you remember my original study?" My response is always, "Do you?"

Teachers are assigned numerous supervision responsibilities. When classes were dismissed at the sound of the bell, a hall proctor would ask several students what they actually learned during a particular class. What unit are you studying in American history or American government, and so on.

Unfortunately, the retention level left much to be desired. "Sit and git," was all too common. Some confessed they got some badly needed rest. One teacher was showing the video, *"Mr. Smith Goes to Washington."* In a class of thirty students, not one student was viewing the film! Most were on their iPod! The teacher was engrossed in her computer at the side of the room.

The author gathered twenty of the school's top students including merit scholars. Together, we produced a video of their four years as high school students. Most confessed to a "hunt and peck" approach to numerous classes.

They confessed to having "shared homework" in many of their factually based classes. Every student expressed a sincere desire to master a "skill" rather than memorization. Solution? Begin with the affirmation that the "jeopardy" approach has little lasting retention.

Class advisory groups can be invaluable for workable ideas. Students have always picked and chose whatever it is they wanted to learn. Test scores are not a valid evaluation of the measure of learning. Students enrolled in the author's American government class, produced an original drama that was presented to the entire school. They won the school districts grand award. Every scene was written and performed by the students.

An American history class also produced a pageant enjoyed even by the PTA. Everything involved in these productions were constructed by the students themselves. Effective? They earned the highest scores in the district's criterion reference tests.

Chapter 4

Student Creative Studies

A GAY MARRIAGE . . .

These two studies indicate the tremendous creativity within students. The only assistance from the instructor was a letter on school stationery indicating this was a study for a school assignment. Some students involved the cooperation of the local police department. It was refreshing to see these students present their original discoveries to the class.

Homosexuality is one of the most explosive issues of our day. The issue either draws acceptance or outright rejection. In the Middle East, gays are subject to death or severe penalties. Most of us are familiar with the Westboro Baptist Church in Topeka, Kansas. Rev. Fred Phelps was notorious for his anti-homosexual rhetoric: picketing funerals, high schools, churches, etc.

Students who were in their final stages of affirming their sexual preference were especially sensitive to this issue. We all know that after extensive studies, there is no definitive genesis of this condition. A junior student desperately attempting to escape the stigma of homosexuality actually rammed a fireplace poker into his stomach. Another student slashed her wrists and came within five minutes of dying. She preferred death to a life of being a lesbian. Other gay students had their tires slashed, their convertible tops cut, ostracized in the lunch room, and many other acts of aversion.

Into this atmosphere, two junior boys concocted a unique and creative study to test the acceptance of gay marriage. Their plan was to visit the area's leading jewelry stores in an attempt to purchase wedding rings for their upcoming nuptials. Several students would act as customers in the store to tabulate the responses of the salesperson. The dilemma was the boys were to appear gay and in love. Neither young man was gay. One was short and heavy and other was tall and slender. Looking at them would convince anyone that "love is blind." After examining a selection of rings, they would jot down the price and its name of the set.

Minutes later, they would return to the store armed with a letter on school stationery, which stated this had been a study. A male salesperson approached them for service. They informed him of their imminent wedding and requested to look at rings. The sales person promptly excused himself for a moment with the information that they might have just what they are looking for. The confederates heard a wide range of homophobic comments. Several other employees suddenly found something to do near the "couple." The ring set called "autumn gold" appeared which was just what they wanted.

Something strange happened for which they were not testing. One ring was for the bride and the other was for the groom. The salesperson gave the groom's ring to whomever was more aggressive or did most of the talking. The "couple," hand in hand promised to return unless they found a more appropriate set. Price was no object.

As soon as they left the store, several sales people enacted a homophobic act mocking the "gay" couple. Their comments and reactions were tabulated by their confederates. Upon return, the couple presented the letter on school stationery indicating all of this was a study.

How did you feel about these circumstances? "Oh, business is business; a sale is a sale. Sexual orientation makes no difference to me whatsoever."

Imagine the discussion when the two students presented their study to the class. Both of the young men are now happily married with children of their own. One is a Baptist minister; the other, a prominent musician. Each wears an appropriate ring. How creative! How unique! How meaningful!

Nothing succeeds like success. Creativity is downright contagious. Listening to the results of "the ring study" inspired two young junior girls. Fortunately sociology provides a mechanism to repeat a study duplicating the identical circumstances. Technically, this is called a statistical comparative study. That term will come up again. The teacher always finds it difficult to deny the aspirations of students. What to do?

Both young ladies came to the teacher's room the day before descending on the identical jewelry stores. A little voice inside the teacher warned of impending doom. Both were very shy. We began an intensive practice:

> "We met in San Francisco. We are very much in love. We want to look at wedding rings."

They got a little more believable with each practice. To be honest, the teacher never felt the girls could pull this off. They received the same official letter stating this was a study, your reaction, etc. They had confederates in the store to observe. The students were obviously attempting something that exceeded their level of comfort. Practice does not always make perfect!

No amount of practice could have prepared them for what actually happened! As they browsed the show cases of rings, a female salesperson approached them to offer assistance. The two students absolutely froze in fright. No doubt their timidity was taken to cover their "secret." With great embarrassment, fear, hesitant sentences, they finally managed to finish their request and announcement of their intention to marry.

The saleslady made it even more difficult for them. She grasped their hands and said in a low voice:

> "Oh, you're lovers. How nice. You should have stayed in San Francisco; they are much more tolerant about this sort of thing. Now don't be nervous honey, I'm gay too!"

Both students made a quick exit and forgot all about the official letter of explanation. Their single question to the instructor was: "Do we have to return to that store???" Student discussion was highlighted by the nature of "coming out"; characteristics of the salesperson. In that academic environment, the two young ladies were perfectly at ease and frankly wished they had stayed and finished their project.

STEALING FROM GOD

Honesty is the best policy. Most of us say that but do we really mean it when push comes to shove? With the store manager's permission, students have visibly stolen merchandise in the presence of other customers. Only one customer openly admonished a student to return the merchandise or she would call the manager. Brazenly, the students walked out but no one reported them. Empty threats!

Then a student made an appointment with the sociology teacher at the conclusion of the school day to discuss her potential study. "Kathy" was an attractive young lady with a high degree of creativity. Her proposed study was to steal the collection plate during the Sunday church service. The teacher's response was that it sounded very original but no church would ever permit that! What on earth are you trying to prove? Her response was simply, "Will people get involved when they see an injustice taking place right in front of them?" The teacher expressed some legitimate negative concerns.

Kathy merely said she had an appointment with the minister of a Presbyterian church about six blocks from school. Certainly this was creative but no minister would allow this during his Sunday service! Within an hour, Kathy returned with the exciting news that the minister approved and would even cooperate! No one would be told of her study—not even the ushers. It was planned for the next weekend for the main service. As a bonus, the minister would prepare a sermon admonishing the congregation of their responsibility to get involved. Their Christian faith demanded it.

With a few student confederates in the church, Kathy made her entrance carrying a brown grocery bag and sat near the front. Parishioners sat on both sides of Kathy. As promised, the minister gave a near fire and brimstone sermon on involvement. He concluded with, "Now, please give your generous love offerings for the needs of the church."

The ushers placed the plate at the ends of each pew. Kathy thanked the person next to her, bent down and dumped the entire plate into her grocery bag. Then she handed the plate to the person on the other side. She stood up, shook the bag, and said a polite, "excuse me." She proceeded to walk out of the church in full view of the congregation. No one apprehended her. The class discussion was absolutely electric. She had expected someone in the congregation to apprehend her and so did the minister. Naturally all the money was returned.

Creative activity is contagious. Enrolled in the class was a young man who had no intention of passing the class not even with a D−. After the discussion, Steve asked if he could rerun that study. He even knew it would be a statistical comparative study. The teacher did not give his request much thought in view of his history of non-involvement in the class before. In addition, he didn't look honest!

It came as a complete surprise when a minister called that weekend to see if this was really an approved assignment. To the teacher's surprise, the minister was enthusiastic about it. Steve made all of the arrangements; he even gathered the necessary student confederates. He armed himself with the official letter from the teacher. He carried a brown grocery bag just like Kathy.

The church was a Baptist Church about ten miles from school. The minister gave the usual involvement sermon admonishing the congregation to "get involved." At its conclusion, the worshippers were encouraged to donate their love offerings to God. Steve sat in approximately the same place as Kathy with parishioners on either side of him. When the usher presented his pew the plate, he dumped the contents in his bag, gave the plate to the person next to him, got up, and said, "excuse me." Members of the congregation silently mouthed to the ushers "he stole the collection money."

Two ushers walked swiftly to catch Steve. Steve hit the front door but hid on the choir steps. Out of sight, the ushers said to each other, "That son of a bitch stole the collection and got away with it." But wait, it doesn't end there.

The following day, the teacher was summoned to the principal's office. "Tell me one of your students didn't steal the collection money during the service?" "As a matter of fact, yes!" Just then the phone rang. The principal shouted at the teacher, "This is for you, explain what you did." A high-pitched indignant woman screamed, "Are you the so-called instructor that is teaching his students to steal?"

"Well ma'am, I am the teacher, please explain what is the problem?" "I was there, I saw it all. Your student stole the whole collection. It is a disgrace." "You said you were there and saw it all?" "Are you deaf, you ought to be arrested." "If you were there and saw it all, what did you do? Ma'am, what did you?" Click, she hung up! By the way, one of the members of the congregation was one of our school bus drivers. To this day, she refuses to speak to me. I hope it is a matter of shame and not hatred.

MISCELLANEOUS STUDIES

The list of creative studies is almost endless. By this time you get the picture. In addition to the studies described above students also sold invisible fish at a local mall; they "shot" a local judge who was a guest speaker in the class. Identical twins were involved. They dressed alike, used the blank gun from the track coach. One twin hid in the adjacent bathroom as the other rushed in and fired three shots at the judge and fled. When "processed" students heard one shot; two shots; as many as five. They apprehended the wrong person.

Even the judge was amazed at this creative incident. Unfortunately, in today's climate this study could never be duplicated. It will just be a matter of time for some students to come up with something similar. Students put a container of coins with a sign above them: "Free, help yourself!"

On a Friday night the box was placed outside of the largest food store in the area. Only a little more than a dollar was taken. People respond differently to an inconsistent situation. Would you send a Christmas card to someone you do not know if they sent you one? Would you accept a ticket from a police officer stating that you were guilty of walking too fast in a local mall!

Why were the DA, the FBI, and the postal inspectors hunting for the teacher?? Without the knowledge or approval of the instructor, a student sent out forty-one racist letters. He even rented a postal box for any responses. When the details of this study were discovered, the entire community celebrated its conclusion: no racism. The DA was so impressed with this study that he became and remains a friend of the teacher. It even made the front page of the local newspaper!

An articulate woman appeared in the class as a critic of the teacher. She addressed the class telling them that the so-called creative teacher was a disgrace to the profession. She even stated that the teacher's contract was now under review by the school board. Who did the students support? The woman made up statistics indicating the class had no educational value and needed to be terminated. To a person, students defended their teacher and also the creative assignments.

Several students demanded to return to the next hour for continued discussion. The teacher's home phone rang repeatedly that night. Parents wanted to know how they could help. Support groups were forming. The class was never told that this was not for real. Who knows, she might return the next year with the same message!

It is difficult to believe that those and many other original studies came from high school juniors and seniors. With no assistance from the instructor, those students exercised an innate creativity to explore some aspects of our social life. The quality of their work can be seen in comparison to the most prominent professional experiments. This is not to say that they are their equal by any means. It does show that these students are on the same road that led others to such significant achievements.

Education is not like a formula, but resembles more of a journey, a way to go. Both the students and the experts used the same scientific method:

1. Hypothesis, that is, state of the problem.
2. Plan the research: choose one of the ten kinds of studies.
3. Collect the data, that is, when and where.
4. Analyze the data, that is, arrange the findings.
5. Draw some conclusions.

With the aid of a computer, look up these "Social-psychological experiments you would never believe." They are

1. Ash Conformity Test: an ingenious method to test conformity through group pressure.
2. The Marshmallow Experiment: what are the long-range effects of deferred gratification?
3. Robert's Cave: how does one establish bonding in diverse individuals?
4. Ape and Child Raising: Conducted in 1931 by Dr. Kellogg and his wife. They raised their son, Donald, with a female young ape to study the effects of socialization.

5. Beneficial Brainwashing: Even the CIA became involved. Ultimately, it came down to a piece of paper on the floor!
6. A Class Divided: Jane Elliott's famous brown eyes versus blue eyes segregation to achieve a racial experience for an all-white third grade class in Iowa, following the assassination of Dr. Martin Luther King.
7. The Monster Test: what are the effects of positive and negative reinforcement?
8. Carlsbery Social Experiment: can people accept an unfamiliar situation?
9. The Philip Zimbardo Prison Experiment: this will be discussed later in greater detail.
10. The Stanley Milgram Experiment: this "shocking" experiment is especially relevant as we study the effects of violent games and movies.

One of the senior boys was especially talented with a camera. We had just studied the nature and effect of the subliminal on the human mind. The student requested fifteen minutes of each of the five classes. "Trust me," was the only justification for his request. He showed up with an 8 mm film which he proceeded to show. It was simply a sunrise to a sunset. Students and the instructor were to write their reactions. Unknown to anyone, he had spliced a picture of a baby, a young boy, an adult man, finally an elderly man, at various parts of his film. What did this remind you of?

Over half the class, the teacher included, wrote that it reminded them of a person growing up and reaching old age! That study bore a resemblance to the beneficial brainwashing study. That student used his innate creativity and photographic skills to provide a very original and authoritative experiment. He now owns his own photo business and is professionally doing very well.

Each student study highlighted some social norms to discover something new or different. Whoever said teaching cannot be a mutually enjoyable experience? Parents began to question the class itself. They firmly believed that school just could not be that enjoyable. Think of all the world's problems that only creative minds can solve! "Read and recite, tell and test" or "sit and get" are not only ineffective, but also counterproductive.

In fairness, it must be stated that several parents visited the class "unannounced" with the intent of finding a disorganized class! What they found was what they did not expect. Several volunteered to help in any way they could. We were lucky to find several with pickup trucks when we needed them for our garage sales!

Chapter 5

Come on In . . .

Guest Speakers

Like the movie, *Field of Dreams*, "if you invite them, they will come!" Guest speakers become a living textbook. They represent whatever profession students want to enter. Real-life experiences make a lasting impression on students. Professionals will not only come, they will become regulars every year.

It was Woodrow Wilson's contention that the primary purchase of education was to prepare students for a productive and meaningful life in society. Someday all the professional posts in our community will need to be replaced. Their positions will be filled with the very students now being prepared for a life of service. Invite these professional individuals to share their expertise and expectations. They will not only come but also come regularly. No less than seventy responded positively each semester—sometimes even more!

When choosing a lawyer, we first inquire about his win/loss record. The same is true of selecting a medical doctor. It would be absurd if we chose someone who lost the majority of his patients. No matter what the expertise of the teacher, he/she is viewed as a dispenser of "book knowledge." Few would deny that today's students are "street wise." Sheldon and Eleanor Glueck, leading juvenile delinquent authorities, went so far as to conclude the majority of today's students are in effect raising themselves.

Consequently, why do we bend over backward to shield them from reality? Whatever is in our society within safeguards should be welcomed into our classrooms to share their points of view. There is a wealth of knowledge that teachers cannot adequately tap into or even understand. Bring in the experts. Sociology II averaged a guest speaker a day! The guest speakers are all authorities in various fields. How do you get them? As a rule of thumb, the more notorious, the more willing they are to share their expertise.

Check the list of speakers and some of their credentials at the end of this chapter. As always, it never hurts to ask! Here is just one example to prove this assertion. The author spent numerous years as a volunteer at the Kansas State Prison located twenty-six miles from his high school. He was even given the opportunity to spend a night behind the bars!

No doubt most people have either read or know Truman Capote's book, *In Cold Blood*. It has sold millions of copies; was translated into thirty languages; was made into a Hollywood movie; it is included in the one hundred best books in the United States. That book has become a staple of many English departments in numerous school districts. In a very real sense, the book almost speaks for itself. Trained English teachers point out many of its salient points. Hitchcock and Smith were executed by hanging at the Kansas prison.

Chaplain James Post not only befriended them for several years, but was assigned to sit with them on the day of their execution. This is something required by Kansas law. Post accompanied them both to the gallows, stood beside them—prayed for them. They both trusted Post with many of their innermost thoughts as they approached their deaths. When asked if he would be a guest speaker in my classes, he never hesitated and agreed to an entire day. Most of the students had already read *In Cold Blood*. In all reality, they were unprepared for the eyewitness presentation from Chaplain Post.

He brought paintings, hand made knives; even the chewing gum that Smith spat into his open hand before the hood was placed over his head. No book or movie could equal the impact of this personal experience. His account was so vivid that when the bell rang at the conclusion of the class, NO ONE moved. As the next class began, they knew something special was about to happen. When urged to leave students, some in tears, formed a line and hugged Chaplain Post. No teacher could possibly equal that effectiveness! Living proof that no teacher can equal the authority of a guest speaker.

Post was but one of the seventy plus guest speakers. How is this for a learning experience? The hour consisted of four speakers: Henry Floyd Brown, convicted of murder; the district court judge who sentenced him; a character witness; Warden of the prison where Henry spent fifty-four years! How about another outstanding guest speaker! Hanna Green, the author of *I Never Promised You a Rose Garden* was giving a speech close to the school. The teacher hurried over and asked if she would come to be a guest speaker. She was delighted to be asked. A large part of the school came to the auditorium to hear this famous author.

Following her presentation, her book was the most sought after from the school library. When we get the trust of our students, and they believe we are on their side, a whole new atmosphere develops. Many times students would inform me before class started that I need to mark them absent as this was the only class they were going to attend that day.

In addition to guest speakers, field trips take on a new meaning. This incident will appear embellished but if anything it is under reported. It needs to be said that our high school is located in a wealthy and homogeneous county. The class had just finished a unit on urban housing which included the pros and cons of high rises for poverty stricken families. Sixty-six crowded on a bus to visit the most notorious high-rise, The Wayne Minor apartments. Admittedly, it was a high-crime area.

Arrangements had been made for a police presence during our visit. Unfortunately they were late—very late. Given our time constraints, we began our guided tour without them. Soon the group was ushered into their gym where the group was suddenly surrounded by Black Panthers. Baskets were passed out for our money and valuables. The demeanor of the woman in charge and her high levels of threatening language brought prayers from the teacher's soul.

Finally the police arrived and surrounded the Black Panthers and the group formed a gauntlet to return to the bus. The police recovered the money and valuables. Once safely on the bus, the teacher apologized to the students and frankly in tears invited them to come to the classroom for a "debriefing." There was no doubt in the teachers' mind that his career was about to end.

The exchange with the students was both frank and mature. The teacher left school that evening with the thought that his career might now be over. The next morning the expected summons from the principal came early in the morning. "Ron, where did you go yesterday for the field trip?" The teacher stuttered a feeble attempt to explain. As it turned out, no explanation was needed. The principal had received numerous support calls.

One parent remarked that her child could not believe that people could hate so much. Every student was supportive and grateful for this lesson in life. One went on to become a state legislator and is the most supportive legislator for education and Northwest in particular.

No one can predict any emergency like this. The teacher takes consolation in knowing that the trip was approved; security was provided; no one was required to attend. Likewise with guest speakers, an administrator approves all speakers; students are free to opt out of any subject matter they do not wish to hear; parent permission slips are signed with the clear understanding that some speakers may use objectionable language.

The best example of the support for this program came from a student who was attending a morning wedding. He didn't want to miss the afternoon speaker. He was caught speeding. He merely told the arresting officer that he didn't want to miss a guest speaker. The officer didn't believe him but let him go saying that he had never heard such an excuse in his entire career.

Early in the morning a students came to the teacher's room. Obviously upset he handed the teacher a dollar bill with the explanation that a customer passed it at his work the night before. He then said, "Turn it over, Mr. Poplau." Written all over the back of that dollar bill was several racial slurs plus in big letters, WHITE POWER. It had a phone number to call for the KKK. Let me make this very clear, I have no interest in the KKK or supporting their activities.

The administration approved the Klan's appearance but it had to be away from school. A local church extended an invitation to use their fellowship hall on a Saturday. The class agreed to be there and to be respectful: information not confrontation.

For the sake of balance, a black Muslim spoke at 1 p.m. and the Klan at 2:30 p.m. The police were in attendance but in plain clothes. Fifty black Muslims appeared in the back of the hall. It was one of the educational highlights of the teacher's career. The *Kansas City Star* covered it.

Someone from New Jersey phoned the teacher to complain of this exposure to young people. The person who called had not even read the entire *Star* article. The effect? The reporter soon became the editor-in-chief of the *Star* for the quality of his reporting. When Martin Luther King's father was in town, he and all of King's children were guest speakers in that same hall! You might be asking: how does all this fit into education? Is there a text? How are grades determined?

Yes, there is a text: Horton and Hunt's Sociology text. It is "pure" sociology and like a math text, it never becomes outdated. Twenty percent of a student's grade is determined by class participation. The district's attendance policy of no more than five absences is in force. An approved book report is required of a subject matter relating to the class, for example, law, race, and so on. Students must keep a daily journal on each guest speaker. Those journals are checked every three weeks. There is extra credit but no substitute credit.

Many students visit points of interest in the community. Ten students each semester spent an entire week at the state mental institution. Yes, they lived there for an entire week and assisted with the therapy, especially with young patients. They were the "normal" patients in the SOCS program. Several were guests for a week on a farm in Missouri. How about living on an Indian reservation, the South Dakota Rosebud reservation? Given the opportunity, students do care about their education. To see them excited about their learning is an absolute high. The teacher feels like a doctor who has just saved a life! Any problems with this program?

One of the major problems you will encounter is other teachers. Students want to hear more from a speaker, plus their friends want to hear a speaker that has a special interest for them. My approach is simple. It is very similar to the philosophy of Gandhi: you must accept the rules about attendance and tardiness. It is your choice.

Our school has what is referred to as a Code Six program. With the permission of each of the student's teachers, they can be gone for part of or an entire day for an approved activity. Some Code Six activities begin as early as 7:00 a.m. Many teachers view their classes as indispensable. Two students came to the teacher for permission to hear a panel of prisoners. The teacher's response always is "if you can get out, you can come in." This particular request was made in March. They had been in that English class since August. They requested a written permission from the teacher.

Again, the teacher's response is simple "if possible." The teacher asked for their English teacher's name. Their response, "It is a woman." After more than a semester in that class, they did not even know the name of the teacher!

Positively the most outlandish incident occurred involving a senior boy. A man in a wheelchair was having problems with his bathroom floor. Could we help?

The man had no money to pay for the repairs. Armed with a Code Six form that extended for three days to complete the repair he was finished right on time. When he returned to school, he could not remember what his first hour class was and in what room! For three days he was totally absorbed in his bathroom remodeling. He had put everything else out of his mind. This raises a basic question of how much do we really teach with "read and recite, tell and test?" He sat but never "really got!"

Our school is located twenty-six miles from the Kansas State Prison. The teacher volunteered there for eleven years. As a kind of "bonus" they made numerous educational opportunities available. Every Tuesday evening we were guests of the prison. After a general introduction, each student was paired with a convict and to discuss with. Every thirty minutes the students would rotate to experience a number of individuals and vice versa. Not once did we ever experience a single problem.

In fact, the students discovered that their worst day was in effect the best day for those incarcerated—sometimes for almost an entire life! At Christmas time, students went to a variety of local stores to be given items that could not be sold. They gift wrapped them under the supervision of a VISTA worker and marked them for age appropriateness and sex. At times, the classroom resembled a warehouse!

The reputation of the class spread to other schools in the area. An inner city school called with a unique request. The inner city teacher was concerned about the low academic skills that existed among not only his students but also throughout his building. His request was to bring 125 of his students to our high school and fan them out in the building for our students to model effective education. This would involve most of our school.

Would other teachers permit this interruption? The sociology students were to seek approval from their teachers to have "guests" for almost an entire teaching day. In two days the "visit" was ready. Three bus-loads of inner city students descended on our building; were met by Sociology II students; were taken to classes throughout the building. The author's request was to have at least five students each hour for discussion. When the bell rang, an inner city student entered the classroom and shouted at the top of his voice, "Man that is the best French class I have ever been in."

The author's response was simply, "I'm happy for you but tell me what made it so good?" "When the teacher spoke, they wrote it down!" Many of us would not find that very innovative. Reluctantly, their time was over and they had to return to their own school. One of the Northwest students said to me in front of the class after they visited that inner city school, "Don't you ever ask for a raise! Those teachers had their hands full. They even had to force the students to sit down!" Good news, we teachers all received a raise!

A common reaction to this guest speaker program is a twofold frustration. We must "cover the book" and how can I get so many speakers. In effect, you are covering the book but in a different manner. The author's summer school began two weeks after the regular school year concluded. In the class were many gifted, highly motivated students. Mention was made of the War of 1812. Surprised and unbelieving the top student asked what war was being referenced. She had never heard of that war! A glance at the American history book she had just covered was the greatest proof that "covering" is not learning.

Start small. The program will evolve. Check your students for some possible speakers. Find out what profession their parents represent. If they cannot come (and most will) they can supply you with names of outstanding people. The following professions were obtained by way of students: lawyers, doctors, dentists, psychologists, ministers, youth directors and even a barber who cut a student's hair each hour, including that of the principal. Study period, home rooms, and so on.. ask them all. Like a stone thrown into calm waters, the ripples will expand.

One teacher had a "special" day each month. He felt his students needed a break once a month. Did you ever notice how quickly students make up their work when they have been absent for whatever reason??? Make an appointment with your administrator and receive the necessary permission. It is after all, OUR class, OUR decision for what will make the class interesting and meaningful. How often have we said or heard, "Unless the lead dog changes, the view never changes!" The community is our classroom—let them come in. Exposure doesn't mean approval.

LIST OF GUEST SPEAKERS

This is the list of speakers who have shared their expertise with students for one semester. Most of them are what would be called "regulars" who come at least once a year, sometimes more often. There are others who were invited at the spur of the moment because they happen to be in the area.

1. Robert Atkins ....Warden, Kansas State Prison
2. Convict Panel ....Kansas State Prison
3. Panel of Sex Offenders ....Kansas State Prison
4. Panel of Police Officers ....Three Local Cities
5. Roger Yates ....FBI Agent
6. Mike Mann...Demonstrates the Lie Detector
7. Vince Werkowitz...Sheriff's Office
8. William Clark...Federal Drug Enforcer
9. Panel of Boy-Offenders ....Atchison Correctional Home
10. Youth Center at Topeka...Adolescent Offenders
11. Kent Harris...National Bomb Authority
12. Helen Swan ....Incest Authority
13. SuEllen Fried ....Child Abuse and Author
14. Charlene Whitney ....Shoplifting Author
15. Peter Adams...Local Gang Authority
16. "Wally"..Satanic High Priest
17. Jon Perry .... Undercover Agent
18. "Molly" ....Parents Anonymous
19. Jim Post... Chaplain: Kansas State Prison
20. Henry Floyd Brown .... Spent 54 Years in Prison
21. Sally Halford...Warden: Women's Prison
22. Asa Steen ....Founder of MOCSA: Rape
23. John Bay...Secret Service Agent
24. Air Port Security ....Speaker Varies
25. Thelma Simmons ....Racial Speaker
26. Rufus St. Claire...Racial Speaker
27. Panel of Black Students .... Varies
28. Veeda Monday ....Black Esteem Speaker
29. Gina Hofer ....Adoption Legalities
30. Lee Ann Britain ....Special Children
31. Herbert Walton...District Court Judge
32. Marylou..Rape Victim
33. Helen Hart... Pro-life Nurse
34. Planned Parenthood... Services Available
35. Dr. Peter Cuppage ....Autopsies

36. Dr. Loren Humphrey ....Cancer
37. Panel of Private School Students ....Local Private Schools
38. Bonnie Sawyer and Children ....Home Schooling
39. Pagan Priestess..Nature Faith
40. Panel of Widows ....Death and Survival
41. Carolyn Conklin.. Alternative School
42. School Board Members
43. Barb Karnes ....Hospice
44. Jackie Sherbo ....Cancer Survivor
45. Dr. Steiner ....Dental College
46. Captain David Coy.. US Soldier
47. Alen Edelman...Holocaust
48. Cathy and Jim Kline ....Death of Son
49. Don Bakely ....Poverty
50. Barbara Strausser ....Astrology
51. David Kensie...Psychic
52. Ruby Porter ....Graphology
53. Catherine Shronkwiler ....Palmistry
54. Harrison Cornelius.. Oneida Indian
55. Robert Smith .... Food Inventor
56. Marcia Beal Hamilton...Epilepsy
57. Rosie Bowker..Mental Illness
58. Don Duncan .... Regression
59. KKK Panel ....Racial Issues
60. Black Muslims ....Racial Issues
61. Dr. Jerry Wychoff..Psychologist
62. Aids Victim
63. Good Samaritan Project .... Aids
64. Mother of a Gay Student
65. Dr. John Tibbetts...Media Expert
66. Cindy Muelberger ....Food Assistance
67. Edna Landis ....Crystal Ball
68. Lynn Kaufman .... Suicide Mother
69. Joyce Grosko... Death: Sons
70. The Cancer Connection
71. Panel of Elderly
72. Organ Donation
73. Homeless Persons
74. Religious Leaders.. Life after Death

There were several more speakers who happened to be in the area. Several community people actually team with the teacher to provide speakers who they have heard and recommend. Through them we were able to get Martin Luther King's father and children! Parents feel honored to be able to assist the learning process. The teacher received word that the family discussed the guest speaker's message every night at dinner. Excellent PR!

Chapter 6

The Three Little Pigs

Whether teachers agree or not, the source of many of our cultural values originates from either the textbooks we use or other media. The Supreme Court concluded that the first amendment covered all motion pictures. Brooks admitted his motion picture, *In Cold Blood*, advocated an end to the death penalty. Camera angles alone convey who are the evil persons in the Orson Wells film, *Compulsion*. McClelland's study indicated the values held by twenty-two literate countries were those expressed in their textbooks and media.

As little children most of us remember when we first heard the story of the *Three Little Pigs*. The wolf demolished the first two structures because of their weak construction material. We learned very quickly brick material was the ideal choice for durability. In the words of Lillian Smith, that value was "caught" rather than "taught." Schools have always been the depository of a culture's values. With almost every teacher's edition, teachers are admonished what values need to be emphasized with suggestion how something is to be taught.

Most literate cultures depend on books or other printed materials to pass on the values that permeate the ideas that will produce the needed bonding ties of cohesive sentiments or simply "way of life." George Washington's cherry tree produces the value of honesty so basic to the American civilization. Only later in life, much later, did we discover the real origin of that and many other historical examples.

Myths have become integral to every way of life. Check out the story of *The Trojan Horse*! Even the Supreme Court held that especially motion pictures were covered by the first amendment as ways to cultivate ideas. Many times motion pictures are even at odds with the actual historical facts to disseminate the producer's values.

Few would deny that on the top of the list of needed values in America is the need to accept one another as equals. Bullying, racism, and deception need to be dealt with in the most effective manner possible. Dr. David McClelland (1917–99) performed an excellent study years ago on "how" to produce needed social values. Let's develop this idea further. He singled out three values: achievement, affiliation, and power. The story he used to illustrate how these virtues were taught were "camouflaged" in the way that story is told. In all cases the story was "the same" but emphasized different values.

In the achievement motive the emphasis was on how to build more boats with better construction so they would not sink or tip over. The value of affiliation stressed how much fun the children had working together, cooperating to produce boats. The power motive stressed how one person inspired and led the others. The story in all cases was the same but the value outcome was different.

Here are some original examples of these crucial values gleaned from a written story. Teachers can improvise their own stories to inculcate whatever values they wish or need.

THE DERBY

The box-car derby was only three weeks away. Mike was nearly finished with his entry. He had planned it for nearly two years. His brother's car had broken down near the last lap of the race. Mike had carefully studied what caused his brother's mishap. He reinforced all the wheels so that the bolts would not break under high speeds. The drive-shaft was also correctly inspected so nothing would jam. Mike treated his "prize" box-car and to his satisfaction it exceeded his brother's speed and with a few minor adjustments it held together very well. "I'm ready for the derby, nothing can beat my entry!" Mike not only won but a company bought his plans to begin duplicating the car for others (the achievement motive).

THE NEW PLAY HOUSE

The new play house came at last! Kids seem to come from all over. Lisa had instant friends. Each offered to help out in any way they could. Denise and Laura carefully took the outer box off revealing a bright white play house trimmed in light blue. Debbie brought her play dishes and two of her best dolls. Karen brought soft drinks for refreshments. Only the cookies were missing. Linda ran home and came back with enough cookies for all of them.

By late afternoon the girls had shared their toys and food. Tomorrow they would play house again. Lisa felt good, it was so much fun playing with all her new friends (values of affiliation).

THE PARK

The park was only two blocks away but few of the children would go there because of John! John was bigger than the rest of the children and liked to push the others around. One of his favorite tricks was to hide behind the bushes and wait until some of the neighborhood children were swinging and throw sand and rocks at them. One day Roger decided that he would not run but stand and fight John. Although Roger was smaller than John, he was determined and skillful. While the other children watched, Roger and John fought by the sandbox. John was easily the stronger and was quickly getting the upper hand. It wasn't long before the other children were inspired by Roger's example and they came to his rescue. John saw that he was no match for all of them and ran away. The children gathered around Roger. Because of him the park now was a fun place for all the children to play (the power motive).

By sheer accident in 1938, the Dani people were discovered in the wilds of New Guinea. Often referred to as "living fossils" or "stone age man," this group apparently existed in this non-literate culture for many years. Their life style was completely devoid of so many technological advancements which today we merely take for granted. These people became a treasure trove for anthropologists. Robert Garner preserved their life style in his famous film, *Dead Birds*, complete with the killing of four Dani people. Edmund S. Carpenter and Marshall McLuhan combined to produce what they termed the evolution of the mind through media.

They introduced television camera, recorded sounds, used Polaroid cameras, and so on. Carpenter's classic, *They Became What They Beheld* is nothing short of an absolute classic.

Technology is at the basis of our way of life. Expressions such as "turn on," "plug in," "picture that," attest to this. Look at an old high school year book to see the rapid cultural change that has happed to each one of us. Few, if any of us, actually check the cash register receipt regardless of how many items we purchased.

In a small town in South Dakota, it was culturally acceptable for girls to dye their hair a different color each week. Boys sported "the thing" which were shirts composed of many different colored materials. It was in effect, a very colorful year! Culture is nothing more than a way of life with supporting ideas. Change the idea and you automatically change the culture.

Observe the parade of changes as you welcome new students: unisex ear rings; body piercing, bagging and sagging probably covered over with an extra-large tee shirt; torn jeans, and so on. Body piercing and some form of tattooing was a staple of the Dani people. Nudity was a phenomenon. If you wore clothing you were in some way ashamed of your body!

Teachers need to become authorities in sociology. One of the finest texts is *Sociology* by Horton and Hunt. The second edition is the finest. Subsequent editions have been "dumbed down." Its publisher, McGraw Hill, went to great lengths to produce a "pure" sociology text. Teachers having this sociological knowledge will have a wonderful source material on how any society is constructed. Let's go back to the Dani people. Consider this: a Dani person makes the first phone call—ever! Photographs are magic.

They are seeing themselves for the first time as they have no mirrors! Recorded voices caused them to run and hide. These were a common reaction of all the Dani persons! Imagine a Dani person on a plane thirty-five thousand feet in the air! By observing them, we can understand the effect of technology on our own lives. The Dani people have never heard classical music. Our human minds have evolved from media of all kinds. Knowing this helps us understand the students we have each year. They will have no concept of what we mean when we say, "Boy, when I was your age!"

McClelland's study on twenty-two literate cultures was the astonishing conclusion: each culture was the sum total of the norms expressed in their books and media! This led George Pettitt to conclude that we are all prisoners of culture. Teachers develop, shape, change, and pass on humanity itself. These are in reality four little pigs: three construction materials plus a cultural value.

Chapter 7

The Fox in the Henhouse

As used in this chapter, the "fox" has no reference to a beautiful woman. The "henhouse" in question houses no chickens. All this refers to a unique police method that enrolled a young looking twenty-two-year-old police officer as a junior with one objective: apprehend students in an illegal purchase of banned drugs within a school during the school day itself. Is this procedure legal? How successful was this after nearly one complete semester?

No one would deny that illegal drug use constitutes a major problem in our society. Our young people are constantly experimenting with a host of illegal substances. As one local police officer stated, "When schools are open, drug sales are up." As a nation we had endured the images of Haight-Asbury in California. 198 acres of "sex, drugs, and rock 'n roll." In addition to that was the "love in" at Woodstock. 500,000 celebrated for over three days.

Too many patrons in the district, the DARE program appeared to be insufficient. Young people were actually shooting peanut butter to achieve a high. Many others were spraying PAM into plastic bags for the same purpose.

The Drug Enforcement Agency at one time appeared hopeless. Their local position was simply education. They did not have the necessary manpower to adequately deal with the growing number of drug abusers. Information was their ultimate weapon. Abusers would be punished. They would be responsible for the consequences of their actions.

These procedures differ from such experiments as that of Jeremy Iverson. At first blush his study might be considered the forerunner of this secret police method. Jeremy was a twenty-four-year-old Stanford University student, who with the approval of the principal, secretly enrolled for a semester at the Mirador High School in California. His objective was simply to gather information and impressions of high school life. The police effort in Shawnee Mission had a dual purpose: observe and eventually prosecute student drug users and pushers. Let's first look at the school where this officer became a fake junior student for nearly an entire semester.

Northwest enjoys a special status within the Shawnee Mission School District in Kansas. The district itself is one of the top-rated districts in the nation. It has produced more national merit scholars than any other Kansas district. Its PTA is especially supportive. During the statewide economic crisis which cut state support substantially, the patrons of the district were willing to increase their taxes than allow their schools to deteriorate. Northwest was conceived as an experimental high school that opened in 1969. It is safe to say that the eyes of the nation were fixed on Northwest's new approach to education.

Visitors from all over Kansas and the nation came to visit the school. It became necessary to use one of the classroom teachers to escort them through the building and explain our approach. Eventually the school was invited to three national conventions: Chicago, Dallas, Little Rock. What were some of these innovations? Students were included in the hiring of new teachers; the PTA was expanded to include students: The PTSA! The school year was divided into three trimesters with the hope and anticipation of becoming a year round school. The curriculum exploded into 212 offerings.

Some classes had a duration of only six weeks, which enabled the students to enjoy a greater variety of teachers' attitudes and methods. A modified block schedule gave the students on two consecutive days an additional forty minutes to study, confer with teachers, or hold assemblies after the school day. A plan's program enabled the students to manage much of their own time. Plan III was almost completely independent. Students and teachers shared the same parking lot and also the same rest rooms. The prevailing philosophy was STUDENTS ARE NUMBER ONE.

Vandalism to the building amounted to a mere $200 for an entire year! One of the graduates, now a distinguished lawyer, attended most of his classes on an irregular basis. Even with this irregularity, he sported a 4.0 GPA! Students were encouraged and rewarded for their own personal motivation. Eventually the school evolved to a National Blue Ribbon School of Excellence. National "search lights" continued to converge on S.M. Northwest.

How are all these accolades germane to this story? On the surface, one would not expect extensive drug use with such an outstanding and sophisticated environment. The "fox" is about to have a feast!

We begin with the enrollment procedure. The sheriff's office provided a fake transcript from a private high school in St. Louis. The fake student was named Tom Collins. Ironically it was the name of a popular alcoholic drink! Here is a major difference from other so-called fake students. Only the district superintendent and the district's lawyer were cognizant of this plan.

No one else was remotely aware of the fox among 2,000 chickens! Many individuals later considered this to be an example of entrapment. Far from it. Tom's instructions were to "buy" not "sell." He gave no one the idea of drug use. Students came to him. All his money was marked by the police department for further evidence.

As a new student, Tom was officially welcomed as a cougar cub. Members of the student government made him aware of the many opportunities available to him. Refreshments were even provided. Everyone learned the school song and school began. Tom casually let it be known that he was in the market for drugs. He would give his commanding officer a weekly report of his findings. The commanding officer posed as his parent. When Tom was absent, the commanding officer wrote his excuses which were accepted without question by the attendance office. Tom also had police work to perform in his city about twenty miles away.

Mr. Joseph Thimes had Tom in his Algebra II class. Thimes was a highly competent and effective teacher. He remembers Tom as a neat dresser and polite with a frequent winning smile. During that part of the class where students work on their own, Tom never worked in class. He did, however, show up the next day with the required homework finished. He later said that he had no idea that math could be so difficult at the high school level. Tom found it necessary to seek the aid of a fellow officer with knowledge in math!

Then, Tom suddenly stopped coming to class. Joe called the "home phone" only to get a recorded message that his call would be returned. As any concerned teacher, Joe sent progress reports to his "home" and asked the counselors to contact his parents. No one could reach him. Tom's picture was not in the year book.

Like so many other high schools, Northwest had a smoking lounge located on the west side of the building. Students and faculty members could grab a cigarette between classes. Unknown to the smokers was an unmarked police van with curtained windows parked in the adjacent parking lot. Smokers would be viewed and taped by a kind of snorkel tube that protruded through the top of the van—a kind of periscope. Students were also viewed and taped running to their private cars where they were observed smoking marijuana. Small pipes were also visible.

The presence of teachers had no effect on the student smokers. The student parking lot was only a short distance from the school building which made it easy for surveillance. At the sound of the bell, students scurried to their various classrooms. Truth can be and often is stranger than fiction. Who would have guessed that drugs and money were transferred during the class. As is often the case with most teachers, they will turn their backs to the class to write something on the board. In numerous classes, drugs and money were passed in a matter of seconds.

Although witnessed by several students, not one student made any effort to report this activity. What drugs were sold, especially at lockers and restrooms: PCP, marijuana, Quaaludes, LSD, Ecstasy, and other miscellaneous drugs. In several cases, the LSD on blotters was nothing but tea! Buyer beware!

As mentioned earlier, Tom was a very handsome man. He became very popular with the girls. Soon invitations to evening and weekend parties at private homes began to include Tom. Most of the time, Tom wore a wire. Many of the "deals" were recorded and later used in court. One party in particular was highly significant. About thirty fellow students attended. In most cases the beer was provided by the parents either free or at cost. All of us know that Quaaludes and alcohol do not mix.

During one party a young girl lost consciousness from such a mixture. The father, not wanting the legal consequences, actually removed a door from its hinges and suggested the girl be transported out of his house and left on the lawn. The conversation was being monitored and a "life and death" decision had to be made which might expose the true identity of the fox. The police had recorded all the license numbers from the parked cars. They were ready to intervene on behalf of the girl when the door opened with the girl on top of the door.

They proceeded to dump her in the front yard and returned to the party. Apparently fear and remorse urged several students to return to the lawn, put the comatose girl in their car and drive her to her home. They left her on the porch, rang the bell and ran. The parents rushed her to the hospital and fortunately she lived. They got her there just in time.

Ironically, the experiment was terminated not over drug sales but because of the sexual propositions by numerous Northwest girls. Early in December, Tom made the formal request to end his undercover work because he felt the growing pressure to "give in" to the numerous girls who almost daily made advances. Tom was withdrawn and his undercover adventure was over. What were the results?

Were drugs a problem at Northwest? How did the students and staff respond when Tom's true identity was revealed? If you sold drugs to Tom on five separate occasions, he built a case against you. In all, Tom built fourteen cases against Northwest students. Arrest warrants were issued and all fourteen were taken into custody. With a live wire, video tapes, and personal experiences, these cases were foolproof. Court proceedings were swift.

Needless to say, the reaction from the students and faculty was mixed. A large number thought it was hilarious! Was this really for real? "I didn't have a clue, he was such a nice guy!" The faculty said little. Only those who actually had him for class ventured a reaction; most were negative on the entire experiment. "Certainly the police have more important things to do."

"Why pick on my high school? I'm sure things are worse in the other high schools." "The image of our school has been tarnished!"

Every case was dismissed! Each parent received a strong letter from the judge urging more supervision. The PTSA who were so outspoken for something to be done, took issue with the whole affair. The students were neither expelled nor were they put on diversion.

The police department was extremely angry. The commanding officer who planned the entire project, became a guest speaker in the author's college class. The officer came close to being totally out of control: the time, the expense, the security risk to the officer! Here is a rather strange and bazaar result: twice a year the commanding officer would be a guest speaker in Northwest's Sociology classes. None of the video tapes could be shown as they became court evidence. "Tom" has since left the police department. He became an outstanding state trooper.

The smoking lounge is now gone. Northwest now has an "electronic fox" viewing the entire building except the restrooms. Now there is a permanent "fox" in the building who has an office directly in the school's mall. The "chickens" are now safe behind closed, locked doors. No metal detectors are in use. Soda cans are outlawed; water bottles need the approval of the school nurse.

Occasionally a student is removed for alcohol abuse; one teacher was caught smoking marijuana over the lunch hour in his car. He was terminated. Test scores are up. The building has an eight million dollar addition; the school now has so many awards and trophies, there is no room to display them. Students and faculty still trade stories about the time we had a "fox in the henhouse."

Chapter 8

Color Blind

There is an important rationale for including this chapter on race. The US Census Bureau reported that 11.5 percent of the US population will move in their lifetime. The greatest percentage of movers will be minority groups. The new translation of IBM has taken on the meaning of "I've been moved!" Home address has become a matter of confusion even for college students. What this now means is the previous schools with few or no minority students have suddenly become integrated. Here is an actual example of what this can mean.

A family of five transferred from a small, homogeneous city to a considerably larger city in Kansas. The children had their first experience attending school with minority students. During a class discussion, one student expressed a strong negative view of interracial marriage. His disapproval would have been objectively considered were it not for the fact that he kept using the "n" word.

That evening at the end of the school day, he was jumped by offended minority students for the racial slur. He was severely beaten and taken to the local hospital. He was unconscious and nearing death. His family withdrew him and began homeschooling as the only remedy. The boy eventually developed a brain tumor!

The author applied at a local community college located near the minority section of the city. The subject he wanted to introduce was black history. The minority section of the city not only opposed a white teacher teaching black history but actually made threats against his hiring. The president of the college visited with the potential teacher and in view of the negative responses asked him if he really wanted to teach this. He openly stated that he just didn't want to get him cut up!

The compromise that was finally agreed to was that the white teacher would park close to the academic building where an armed police officer would escort him to the classroom. The classroom door would have to be open throughout the three-hour class each week. The class was composed of twenty-one blacks and one Jewish student. Only after three sessions did the students began to participate in the class discussions.

The Swedish author, Gunnar Myrdal observed that the source of America's racial problem was due to our statement of equality of all peoples in the Declaration of Independence. Creed and deed are at odds with this basic American document. Most of us are aware of the many historical attempts to achieve racial equality. Schools in general have played an important role in advancing the idea of equality.

Who could forget that horrendous day in April of 1968 when Martin Luther King was assassinated in the Lorraine Motel in Memphis? Schools and cities became a powder keg of the first order. White teachers were especially at risk. Student desks were thrown out of windows. Many teachers sought safety behind locked doors. A neighboring private school just four blocks away was ultimately chosen for what could only be considered total destruction.

Students and female teachers were sheltered in the basement behind locked doors. Each male teacher (including the author) was given baseball bats and stood guard at every entrance. Fortunately the police arrived and successfully dispersed the crowd.

Teachers sought ways to deal with racial matters. Top of the list of concerns was the need for scientific evidence of racial equality. The world was outraged at the details of the holocaust during World War II. Millions of people were exterminated because of their race or nationality. Was there any authoritative study dealing with the issue of human equality? One major one was discovered.

THE UNESCO REPORT OF 1951

The new branch of the UN with headquarters in Paris undertook the most scientific study ever done of race. Every section of the world was invited to send their top authorities on racial matters to Paris. Ninety-six eventually participated in this famous and definitive study. After several years, their preliminary conclusions were published with the invitation to anyone who had disagreements to come to Paris and share them.

Finally, their final report was issued in 1951 under the title of THE RACE CONCEPT. The members of this study met again in Kansas City, Missouri in 1965 to see if any of their conclusions needed to be adjusted in view of modern technology. They republished their conclusions without any changes whatsoever!

Many of the leading textbooks incorporated their findings. Teachers now have that authoritative study to base their attitudes and knowledge on race. The UN building in New York has a huge statue of a completely nude man in its front lobby. This statue represents all human beings regardless of their nationality or culture. In effect, The UNESCO Report states the obvious when the obvious needed to be stated. Here are the main conclusions of that report.

I

All persons belong to a single species, the *Homo sapiens*. Because of this single source there was no separate creation for the each racial group. UNESCO comes very close to stating that there is only one race, the human race, with a variety of variations. Because of this single source, all persons have simple structures, characteristics, and functions. Consequently, there is no special dignity attached to any one race. Well might we say, "I am HUMAN therefore I am proud."

II

RACE: for a characteristic to be deemed racial, it must be something physical and hereditary. In view of this conclusion, there is no Jewish race, no American race, and so on. One can change his nationality or religion as so many people worldwide have done. The definition of RACE was a conclusion that the members were in unanimous agreement. Any other definition of RACE was not scientific.

III

Some physical differences between human groups are due to differences in hereditary constitution and some to differences in the environment in which they have been brought up. Both of these factors can and do affect a person's reproductive genes. Cross fostering of persons from various cultures display the effect of one's culture. Even one's language can affect the shape of one's mouth which in many cases produces an "accent."

IV

Mankind clusters around three major groups. There is no evidence that one group is innately superior to another as sometimes emphasized. Color cannot be an absolute divider of the races. Many of the physical traits overlap considerably. Color is one of these traits that can vary with each racial group.

V

Mental characteristics are not included in the classification of human beings. The normal individual regardless of his race can be educated. The full range of temperament and intelligence exists in every group. UNESCO preferred the word, ETHNIC, to race. Again cross fostering produces a cultural change within groups.

VI

There is no biological argument against interracial marriage. Any bad effects of such a marriage are due to social factors not scientific factors. This conclusion posed the most difficult especially in the United States. Various states had laws banning interracial marriage. Because of PROJECT CLEAR, blacks and whites could fight side by side beginning with the Korean War. A number of American soldiers returned to the United States with Korean brides and in many cases their marriages were not recognized. US citizens for many years were not permitted to marry Native Americans. The United States accepted this conclusion with the understanding that it would be "played down."

In actual practice, how successful is the UNESCO Report? The author's most effective professor would frequently say, "I do not know a generality, I only know a for instance." Almost in the same breath, he would remind us that he had nothing to fear from truth, and nothing to gain from error. On a bus trip to Louisiana in 1965 (three years before the Civil Rights Act) seated next to me was a white young lady. She was engrossed in a magazine article, "I Was On a Glue Sniffing Jag."

When the opportunity presented itself, we struck up a conversation. It soon became obvious that she was an avowed racist.

The slightest indication that the author believed in racial equality, brought a diatribe no publishing company would print! She continually referred to blacks as "things." No one had ever challenged her position. After all, this was the Deep South. We were both very cordial, polite, but radically different. Of course she had no knowledge of the UNESCO

Report—probably never heard of the United Nations either. The trip was long enough for the author to cover in detail all the UNESCO conclusions. She even shared a "snack." She was simply "blown away" with the logic of the conclusions.

When she reached her destination, she was exceptionally courteous. She left the bus, but almost immediately returned and said in parting, "I think you could teach in Louisiana as long as you would like." She hugged and left. Oh, she left her "glue sniffing" magazine on her seat!

The author began teaching in a private school in the inner city. This would be the first experience teaching an American history class consisting of several black students. The author had just returned from a teacher exchange program in Brazil. My initial class in that school consisted of the UNESCO Report. It was an introduction to the Civil War. Reminded of the admonition of "nothing to fear from truth," the author launched into the report as dynamically as possible. Since it was my first class in that high school, the teacher evaluated was in the room!

Call it grace under pressure, it appeared that the author had passed the test. "Appeared" does not, however, mean reality.

A delegation of white students requested an after-school session. They appeared to be somewhat hostile. To a student, the entire class was assembled. A student representative ventured the conviction that any racial information was perceived to be highly offensive since there were black students in the class. "Barbara," a black student rose and stood beside the author. She told the class how refreshing it was to finally discuss race. She publicly endorsed the UNESCO Report. In tears she managed to say, "I am your equal, finally we have proof what we black people have always known! Welcome, Mr. Poplau, I love you!"

It had become a tradition in that school for seniors on the last day of classes, to write on their uniforms/clothing some rather derogatory words or phrases. In an all-school announcement, the principal cautioned the seniors they would be sent home if they defaced their clothing. "Kathy" was definitely the school racist. As a black student, she refused an "interracial home visit." "I will never allow a white person in my house!"

As the senior class sponsor, the author responded to an all call from the school's intercom. "Kathy" was challenging the entire second floor! Racist and other words covered her clothing. Every teacher on that floor merely stood mute in their classroom doors. The author confronted Kathy with expulsion for her conduct. Her response, "This has been going on for 400 years!" "Maybe so Kathy, but not the 401st. You have to leave now," there were no exceptions. She excused herself, went into the restroom, and emerged with spotless clothing. To my great relief, she returned to class. When students deserve us the least is when they need us the most!

The following day, Kathy showed up for graduation practice with her hair up in curlers and short shorts! Again, against the rules. Before practice began, the author informed her that she could not join her class for practice—she would have to return home. Again she went to the restroom. With her hair down and in a long shirt she participated in the rehearsal. That night as she accepted her diploma, she turned her back on the principal. With outstretched arms she came to the class sponsor and said, "Thank you Mr. Poplau, you were fair!"

The UNESCO Report does not include exceptions. "Equal ability, full range of temperament" equal responsibilities. Living proof, "We have nothing to fear from truth," especially scientific proof.

All the numerous affirmative action programs have but one objective: equality status. How many more groups do we need to achieve this? NAACP, CORE, busing, fair housing, job opportunities. We need to begin with the basic premise: All men belong to a single species! Shakespeare's Merchant of Venice, "If you cut us, do we not all bleed?" It is not true that "sticks and stones may break my bones but words will never hurt me." UNESCO's words will help. You have my word on it!

There are many racial activities designed to bridge the cultural differences. Dr. Robert Williams in the early 70s produced an exam he entitled THE BITCH TEST: The black Intelligence Test of Cultural Homogeneity. The test consists of one hundred black expressions. He held that many intelligence tests were culture specific. Most of the black expressions can be accessed on line together with the answers. A very interesting test is the black IQ test. It consists of sixty multiple choice questions to determine one's knowledge of black issues and historical facts.

Fortunately, it also has the answers at its conclusion! Remember: one's IQ does not reveal one's innate ability but simply performance. Northern blacks outscore many Southern whites in examinations such as the Texas Readiness for Reading. Where opportunities are equal, the results are similar.

The SEED program which began in Washington, D.C., is definite proof of the impact of one's environment. The program withdraws black children from their neighborhoods—chosen by lottery not by test scores. They attend boarding schools six days a week. The resulting test scores are some of the highest in the nation. Their graduates excel in many of the most prestigious colleges and universities in America.

As teachers begin each school year, we need to see with our eyes and also with our minds. People are people regardless of color or culture of origin. EACH not EVERYONE is the same. In a good sense "they are all that way: human." Yes, there are cultural differences. A Native American senior boy met with his teacher one day after school. He remarked that he was very confused. He liked and respected his government teacher but had an adjustment problem. "YOU tell me one thing, my parents tell me something different! What am I to do?" It posed a major problem.

They resolved it by comparing the demands of the American system and that of the Native American culture. Knowing BOTH of them, he was free to choose his own set of beliefs.

Again, a good sociology text like the second edition of Horton and Hunt are a major source of so much information about the structure not only of our society but also about the nature of all groups in our society. The question is not, do we have a race problem in this country, but do we have to have one? Psychology states that all people worldwide are born with a tendency to gravitate to tolerance and cooperation. Teachers can and must manifest an awareness of equality. UNESCO states the definite conclusions about the various ethnic groups we find in our communities and therefore our schools.

Prejudice is being down on what we are not up on. Teachers hold the future on everyone. There was a bulletin board close to the entrance of our school that said: MAN MADE FOOTPRINTS ON THE MOON BECAUSE A TEACHER FIRST MADE MARKS ON HIS MIND. Sacred scripture also states: TEACHERS WILL SHINE LIKE THE STARS.

It is O.K. for teachers to be "starry eyed" and believe that the sky is the limit!

Chapter 9

Perspectives on Death

The measure of a life, after all, is not its duration, but its donation.

—Corrie Ten Boom

Establishing a class on death perspectives was not an easy undertaking. The most asked question was some form of WHY? Aren't teenagers sufficiently depressed already? Won't this class add to their depression? The worst question challenged the value of such a class. Once the class actually started, four weeks extended to six and could go even longer. Let's put to rest the suggestion that the need for such a class has no justification.

For years our schools taught such skills as cooking, sewing, knitting, and even sex education. Almost every middle school and high school has woodworking and auto mechanic classes to instill skills. Those in our society who are expecting a child are inundated with possible names, prenatal care, and diets to ensure a healthy baby; sonograms; actual birthing methods; philosophy of child development; even government regulations with mandatory seat belts. The very purpose of education is to prepare students for a meaningful and productive life. We quickly learn that babies do not come with directions or survival skills!

A normal life covers a beginning, a climax, and an ending. The end should never be a "do it yourself event." No matter who we are or how important we think we are, we all have the same ending: death. It is not IF we die, but *when and how!* Over the course of a normal life span, the average person will lose someone close to us. The resulting grief is a universal, individual experience. For all too many it comes as a complete shock. We either have no inner strength or are left helpless.

Junior and senior students who opt for Sociology II class are exposed to every conceivable aspect of death. Perhaps a better name for the unit would be life appreciation. From day one they realize there is a mountain of issues associated with death. The class uses no euphuisms such as "passing away." On day one, each student receives an official death certificate. Their first assignment is to write their own obituary. A sample form is in the end of this book. They can also use those published in the newspapers as a guide. Why is this activity so important at the start of the unit?

Few young people think of their own morality. The time to realize this is when they are young and can look at this experience more objectively. The unit has a cluster of guest speakers. These speakers are real life plus they are eager to share their experiences with young people. The annual list includes

1. A panel of widows and widowers
2. Death by cancer
3. Breast cancer survivor
4. Organ donation
5. Suicide: parent survivor experience
6. Child death by accident
7. Child death by disease
8. Religious leaders: life after death
9. Funeral director
10. Cremation
11. Soldiers: political death
12. Student panel death of parent or family member
13. Hospice
14. Medical doctor
15. Muslim: concept of death
16. Death by murder

Students write a reaction to each guest speaker as part of their assignment. Some speakers are grateful to have the opportunity to share their personal feelings. In fact, students from other district schools request to be on the student panel. This is in effect the first opportunity they have had to share their feelings. In jest, one student asked if he died during the unit would he get extra credit!

Numerous students visit privately after the school day to share personal problems resulting from a death of someone close to them. Some recount "strange sounds," "images," and "dreams." The most asked question, sometimes in tears, "Am I crazy?" "Is this normal?" "Will this ever get better?" They are relieved to simply know that grief is universal. It has no road map. There is growth inherent in grief. Tears result from love. Some prayers refer to this life as a "valley of tears." All of us sooner or later pass through that valley.

These musical masterpieces have death as their major theme. These and many others have been performed for years.

1. Verdi's Requiem—note the shattering dies Irae!
2. Mozart's Requiem
3. Saint Saens: Dance Macabre Mozart
4. Berlioz: Symphonie Fantastique
5. Puccini:: La Boheme
6. Bach: Some Sweet Death
7. Mahler: Symphony #9: Goodbye to the World
8. Franz Liszt: Totentanz
9. Rachmaninov: Isle of the Dead
10. Beethoven: third and seventh Symphonies, second movements.

We also have many cultural expressions referring to death. To list a few:

1. Over my dead body!
2. He would turn over in his grave . . .
3. Death defying act
4. He cheated death
5. Beyond the grave
6. He/she corked
7. Dead as a door nail
8. Drop dead
9. I will go to my grave
10. One foot in the grave
11. Kick the bucket
12. Your number is up
13. Six feet under
14. His/her last breath
15. Pushing up daisies
16. Here today, gone tomorrow
17. Good grief
18. You will be the death of me yet
19. Cigarettes; coffin nails
20. Tombstone pizza

A new phenomenon has given our young people a potential death on a daily basis: school shootings. Let's look at a real example of an unspoken reminder of possible death. An inmate at the Kansas Correctional Institution causally stated to a visiting teacher, "I must be bad, look what it takes to subdue me. A gun is pointed at me every day!" Security measures at our schools convey the inescapable message of potential death that could happen at a moment's notice. These security measures are perhaps the greatest reminder of a potential end of life. "Look what it takes to protect me from a violent death?"

ADVANCE CATASTROPHE TECHNOLOGIES

Attending church services is intended to bring one closer to God. One would not expect attendance at a religious ceremony would put their lives in jeopardy. This notice appeared in church bulletins beginning on March 18, 2018. A diocese in Kansas ran this notice for three consecutive weeks:

> Our insurance company, Mutual of Omaha has sent us a number of procedures to do in case of an emergency. The Archdiocese has asked all parishes to follow these procedures. We are printing for you the following list of things to do if there is an active shooter on the property or at church. Please read and consider these things. Remember as much as possible—number of shooters, location of them, physical description, types of weapons and number of victims. Call 911 as soon as it is safe to do so.

1. Run—Hide—Fight. If you can safely leave do so. Have an escape route in mind, leave your belongings behind, keep your hands visible.
2. Hide—make sure you are out of the shooters' view, block entry to your hiding place, lock the door, silence cell phones, remain in place until released by law enforcement.
3. Take action—only as a last resort. Attempt to incapacitate the shooter, act with physical aggression, look for items to throw at the shooter or use missals to throw at him.

> When law enforcement arrives, their first priority will be containing the shooter, not helping victims. Do not stop officers to ask for help or directions when evacuating. Evacuate the premises as quickly as it is safe to do so. Remain calm and quiet. Follow instructions. Keep your hands visible at all times.

As one enters the church, a large sign reads: watch your purse, not everyone comes here to pray. One Sunday during the service, a man dressed like Merlin, the magician, carrying a huge stick, walked up the center aisle and stood in front of the main altar. Not knowing what to expect, some parishioners froze while others sought protection. Fortunately, he left without causing any disturbance other than a distraction. Prayers were intense!

Motion pictures are saturated with death. *Natural born killers* drew an outrage from various sources for its portrayal of violent death. Another recent film, *Django Unchained* brought similar outcries for its depiction of death.

One of the class exercises that the students especially enjoy is drawing their concept of death. Most pictures reveal some awareness of an afterlife. Even the colors the students' chose have a significance. The color wheel can be found on line. Each student explains the meaning of their illustrations. Their choice of colors coincides with their explanation given on the color wheel: energy, spirituality, sadness, danger, hope, peace. All assignments and class activities are given to each student at the end of the unit.

Highly recommended for classroom viewing is the 1984 Hollywood movie, *Silence of the Heart.* The acting is superb. The film masterly covers the causes of suicide. The boy's death occurs during the first part of the film. The remainder reveals the causes that no one picked up on. Why the boy committed suicide is not revealed until almost the final moment of the film. It is an excellent means to introduce the speakers whose son or daughter took their own lives.

The death of a student is always tragic. A terminal disease can be a "teachable moment." Schools are very similar to one's family. Some of the students have been together twelve or thirteen years. Silence is not golden. The dying student wants his or her life to serve some purpose. They strive to create a legacy. These students became a major, integral part of the school. In effect, the entire school shared in their dying process. No matter what the subject matter, classes always began with an update on the students' death progression.

The students in turn shared their fears, hopes, and even the acceptance of their condition. Eventually when the students' condition kept them from attending school, classmates volunteered on a daily basis to visit and assist with assignments. When they died, permission was granted for anyone to attend the funerals. The church was crowded. With all the advance involvement, students and faculty bid farewell to a "family member." Their lives were enriched by this experience. What follows is the life and impact of these three who will never be forgotten.

ALLYSON WOODBURY

December 1988—April 2007

"Live Strong"

Born in December of l988, Allyson was a member of the Shawnee Mission School District and lived in Kansas all of her eighteen years. Gifted, talented, sensitive, and outgoing could describe this young lady. Her mother was an employee of the district. She was one of those students who would be on a short list to be the most likely to succeed. Allyson excelled in dance and spent many hours practicing. This graceful and at times vivacious activity fit her personality.

The fall of 2002, her eighth grade year, brought some concern over a developing pain in her shin. Her dance activity on that particular day exceeded three hours. "Mom, I just overdid it, I'll be fine." As might be expected, her mother applied all the home remedies any concerned parent would attempt: rest and pain relievers, but the pain remained constant and persistent. "We better have our doctor take a look at it just to be on the safe side." The x-rays showed nothing out of the ordinary.

Only after an MRI did the family doctor refer her to a specialist. Two weeks was the earliest he could see her. As the mother was about to hang up the phone, she inquired what was the specialty of this new doctor? To her absolute devastation she learned he was an oncologist! President Kennedy called it "grace under pressure" to explain what ensued. Four days later came the dreaded news: cancer. Ewing's sarcoma, childhood cancer of the bone.

Because of her young age, the doctor was confident that she would be successfully treated. He gave her about a 70 percent chance of beating it. Sixteen chemo treatments plus a bone salvage surgery left her cancer free. For the moment she was home free. However, in her junior year at Northwest her cancer returned. Allyson's condition was shared by her classmates. In a sense they suffered with her. Her struggles with this disease were also a part of their lives. "There but by the grace of God go I!" However, another problem arose: her health insurance was reaching its limit.

Allyson's life motto was LIVE STRONG. Northwest students began to mobilize to help their "family member." They sold bracelets at school and the community. They contacted Lance Armstrong who agreed to a personal phone call of encouragement. Students put together a video tape and sent it to the Oprah show. As Charles Spurgeon wrote, GIVING IS TRUE HAVING. Allyson went to Washington, D.C. in an attempt to procure increased funding for muscular/skeletal research.

She became an advocate for the Dream Factory—the Children's Miracle Network. Her motto of LIVE STRONG was eventually tattooed on her right hip. She had signed up Northwest's community service class. The teacher began to make all the necessary adjustments. When her mother was asked what the school could do for Allyson, her response was simple and to the point. Do anything that would keep her life as normal as possible. It was Richard Wright who wrote, "How can I act normal when I am thinking about acting normal?"

Alternate assignments were made plus a double set of textbooks were given to her to relieve her of the weight of carrying so many books. She kept up, she did not slack off. In many cases she outdid her own classmates. What might sound unusual to some is that Allyson did not perceive herself as anything but normal.

Students wanted to be informed of the progress of her disease. Discussion before and after class centered on her condition. The number one question was a simple: how can we help? It is only fair to say that some students shied away from Allyson. A few students thought that her disease was contagious. Like the common cold, they could catch it. For most of the students this was a very vivid lesson in life. Elbert Hubbard said it best, "The love we give away is the only love we keep!"

Allyson was an attractive young lady. The traditional Northwest homecoming celebration was coming soon. Students were busy planning the usual activities but not too busy to overlook Allyson. Queen candidates are chosen by numerous student clubs and activities. Under normal conditions, Allyson would have been a likely candidate. She was chosen almost unanimously to be the homecoming queen. By this time Allyson was in a wheelchair. The crowning took place during the evening football game.

The outpouring of love, affection, and concern, permeated the entire crowd. Cheers of "Allyson, Allyson" rocked the stadium. It was a night to remember and cherish.

Her cancer had developed to the point of no return. Other experimental procedures were tried but had no effect. She wanted so much to live, to graduate and to attend college. The Oprah program never materialized nor did she receive a personal visit from Lance Armstrong. Only four months of life remained. On April 7, 2007, Allyson died.

The wake was certainly a celebration of her life. The teacher's intention was to simply sign the book, offer condolence to the family, and just fade away. The students had transformed the funeral home into a sea of pink, Allyson's favorite color. Memorial pink signs surrounded the school, inside and out.

Young people who die will remain at that age forever, especially in the minds of the parents. In this case, Allyson will never vote, never marry, never have children, never have a career. We can only guess what might have been. Every April 15 the parents are reminded that their child is legally gone—no longer a tax deduction. No one can or will ever understand why some young people live such a short life.

Another grieving parent was a guest speaker at Northwest during the unit on death. About halfway through the class, she screamed at the students. She shouted how much she hated them. She kept saying over and over again, her daughter was "better than any of them!" She sat at the teacher's desk and began to cry. Students understood and one by one they hugged her. "In youth we learn; in age we understand!"

Through all the pain and what appeared to be an imminent death, Allyson had been making plans to attend college. After the funeral, the mother was checking Allyson's cell phone. It had two returned calls from colleges. They wanted to share with Allyson whatever the requirements would be for her to enroll. A pink plaque was placed in some nearby shrubbery close to Northwest High School. Not only did it have her name and dates but also her life's motto: LIVE STRONG.

Live as if there is no tomorrow
Laugh because it helps our heart
Love because it's all that really matters.

In the words of Benjamin Franklin: "Lost time is never found again." Short or long, time is the circumference of all our lives.

Chapter 10

Byron Andrew Grosko:
July 30, 1965–March 29, 1983
Sean Joseph Grosko:
February 11, 1969–May 7, 1985

Any man's death diminishes me because I am involved in mankind.

—John Donne

Some people become role models for others. In grade school art classes, students trace artwork to make exact copies of the original. So it is with people. The South Africans have a special word that conveys the significance of human role models: UBUNTU. The English translation expresses the nature and extent of role models: "I am because you are!"

The life of Bryon and Sean Grosko ultimately inspired not only their classmates but the entire nation as well. During class reunions, graduates invariably remark many years later: "I was in Byron Grosko's class." Afflicted with Duchene's muscular dystrophy, Byron was confined to a wheel chair and had very limited mobility. His mother, Joyce, had been an effective speaker in numerous college classes on the needs of exceptional children.

The nature of the disease guarantees an early death. Like any concerned parent, Joyce wanted every service the high school could extend to her sons. If Byron or Sean enrolled in sociology, he would most likely die during the class itself. Also, his presence might disturb other students during the extensive unit on death and dying. All of these concerns were futile. On the first day of sociology, Byron said to the class, "Do not be concerned about me, I have a lot to learn and a lot to share."

Byron's main objective was to graduate with his classmates. Fortunately the entire school had wheelchair access. However, Byron was not reticent about asking for needed assistance. He wanted a group of strong boys to help him and his mother early in the morning. His mother could no longer lift him

59

from the bathtub and put him in his wheelchair. In fact, she suffered from a herniated disc trying to lift both of her boys.

Byron's brother, Sean, also suffered from Duchene's muscular dystrophy. Thinking of his mother's plight, Byron requested assistance from each of his seven classes. Surprisingly the students created a calendar to schedule their mornings with Byron. Word spread to the neighboring high school. They too agreed to help.

It was not uncommon to have a houseful of students at one time!

Classmates also made carbon copies of class notes to relieve Byron's inability to write extensively. Many students carried his schedule of classes in the event of a fire drill or any other emergency. It was not uncommon to see several students carry Byron down the stairs for assemblies. All this seemed to be just normal.

Byron had a fondness for sports, especially football. Almost at every home game, Byron was on the field next to the football team. It was reminiscent of Ronald Reagan's "win one for the Gipper!" As a result of his support, one of the most touching and memorable incidences occurred the night the quarterback was named the "big man on campus." Without any hesitation, he removed the crown and placed it on Byron's head. The room erupted like a thunder clap. The chant began, "Byron, Byron." They honored him as the true big man on campus.

Something else happened–Byron fell in love. He insisted that his mother only pack a lunch that would not cause him to dribble. In tears the young lady came to the teacher's room saying, "It's not fair, it's not fair." She did agree to attend the school dance with Byron. She pushed him around in his wheel-chair as if they were dancing. By this time the students were well versed in taking care of Byron. All this attention seemed to be normal. Byron elicited skills and feelings students never knew they had. He was their mentor without even knowing it.

Only once did Byron complain to the teacher about his condition. One morning Byron came unexpectedly to the classroom and kept saying, "This is not fair! It is not fair what my mom has to go through." No tears, only emotion surfaced as he said he was beginning a routine of psychic healing. "One of these mornings I'm going to come to your room early. Then I am going to step out of my wheelchair and demolish it in front of you." Secretly, I bet that he would do just that.

Although his mother was not aware of the attempt to help him, his father agreed to take him to the healing priest, Father D'Orio. Father D'Orio was in Kansas City with a healing crusade at the city's largest arena. The priest filled the area on two separate days of healing. There was a special section up in front of those in wheelchairs. Both Byron and Sean were in the front row. Byron was absolutely speechless when the priest blessed and anointed him.

Although disappointed, Byron remained resigned to the fact that his suffering would continue. The desired miracle never happened. His disappointment was not for himself but for all those who were helping him.

Now it became a race against time. His body weight was below one hundred. He was in and out of the hospital numerous times. Graduation wasn't too far away. It would not be an exaggeration to say that several students achieved graduation because of his inspiration. The night before he died, he consented to a taped interview. He confessed that he was in no way cheated. He felt good about his life. Once again he expressed concern for his mother and brother. Under no circumstances was his brother to come to the hospital. His condition would only be a dress rehearsal for his brother!

The dreaded call from Joyce came shortly after 10:00 a.m. Byron had just died. She asked that the author come to her house after school. From the unit on death, Byron had planned his entire funeral. The music he selected was recorded on a special tape to be played at the funeral home. He asked the author to give the eulogy. He added, "Do a good job!" Standing next to the casket on top of an open grave makes it difficult "to do a good job." Hundreds of students and faculty members gathered near the grave.

Byron had become a Northwest legend. He had one final surprise, a climax only he could have planned. As the casket descended into the grave, the author pressed the play button on the boom box placed on top of a tombstone. The massive sound of the London Symphony Orchestra filled the cemetery with the theme from *Star Wars*! Students hugged, wept, smiled. What Byron was saying in his last hurrah: "I'm free, I'm no longer confined by a weak and dilapidated body. Thank you. Thank you!"

On graduation night that May, Byron graduated posthumously from Shawnee Mission Northwest. As his name was read, the students instantly rose as if to honor him one more time. While they were cheering, a star fell in the sky. Byron was saving for the final time, "I'm O.K., thanks."

As a tribute to this outstanding young man, *Reader's Digest*, published a lengthy story of his life and what it meant to others. Two movie scripts were written on Byron and also his mother. In the words of Oscar Wilde, "Memory is the diary we all carry about with us." As this young man, this mentor of others, said: "I have a lot to learn and a lot to share."

Byron's brother, Sean, inherited the love and concern of the entire student body. Byron had prepared us all very well. Sean now enjoyed many of the same gestures bestowed on his brother. Sean's last request was to "go someplace warm" before he died. That was all he had to say. The entire school enlisted the generosity of the community in their effort to make his dream a reality. They approached World Airlines for three complimentary tickets: one for Sean, his mother, and his best friend, Shannon. The destination: Hawaii, "someplace warm."

The pilot even permitted Sean to sit in the cockpit to watch the plane land. Over 1,000 dollars was wired to their hotel for any expenses. As their boat encircled the islands in the warm breeze, Sean looked lovingly at his mother and said, "Oh mom, this is the life!"

Sean was a devoted Kansas City Royals baseball fan. Sitting on his mother's lap, he appeared to be in a prophetic coma and shouted, "They, won, they won, for me!" The Royals were playing a strategic game in Canada. The outcome would determine if they would make it to the World Series. The Royals were assembled on the field. They were informed that a little dying boy in Kansas had seen them not only win this strategic game, but saw them also win the World Series. Sean's spirit permeated every player as they beat the Toronto Blue Jays by their widest margin to date!

The rest is history: down by the first three games, the Royals rallied to win the remaining four. They did indeed win "for him!"

Sean died on May 7, two days after the author's birthday. The day after he died, a pineapple arrived from Hawaii. That was the most delicious pineapple ever! His mother wrote the following:

> A skinny kid who died in peace and in courage, who gave his all to us. Goodbye Sean my darling, my son.

These were but three of the "family" members who died during the school year. Three Northwest students attempted suicide during the school day. An American government girl who tried to kill herself outside the author's classroom door. Her reason: She was not passing. When our district leveled out at 40,000 students, the statistics were more than a concern:

1. Twenty-four students died each year on the average.
2. Two hundred fifty students experienced a death in their immediate families.
3. Twenty percent of students lost a parent.
4. The divorce rate from the loss of a child is high.
5. The average American has a life expectancy of about 30,000 days.

During a spring break, a student died of mysterious circumstances. Those with him would only say that he accidently fell into the river and drowned. No one would give any further details. The mother of the boy's best friend called late that night to inform the teacher that Ted had never seen a dead body. Tomorrow will be his first experience. He was sitting lighting one match after another. "Recommend something, I am really afraid he might hurt himself."

A call to the funeral home arranged a private viewing the next morning before the scheduled public wake. They would have four men close by in case Ted became violent or out of control. The teacher picked up Ted the next morning and drove him to the funeral home for a private viewing. He slowly walked down the aisle, stopping frequently. When we reached the casket, Ted went into shock. He made an effort to rearrange his friend's hair. He cupped both his hands over his mouth to squelch a scream.

After what seemed like hours, the teacher took Ted to McDonald's. One of the fondest memories any teacher can have occurred during our fast food lunch. Ted looked at the teacher with the utmost reverence, gratitude, relief, peace. His first spoken words will never be forgotten. "Thank you, Mr. Poplau, I would never have been able to have done this without you. You showed me that you cared about me and also my friend."

His friends arranged for a rock concert at the school's auditorium. Ted has gone on to live a normal life. During that luncheon, the teacher resolved to offer a class on death to help others deal with one of life's tragedies. Judging from the comments and letters from graduates, it was a good decision.

Chapter 11

Blue Skying

Knowledge is like a candle. When you light your candle from mine, my light is not diminished. It is enhanced and a larger room is enlightened as a consequence.

—Thomas Jefferson

Frequently as young people, we would lie in an open space and observe various cloud formations. We would discern a pattern or image of something real. We began to think of a distant future and even ways to achieve it. Some would call this day dreaming or wishful thinking. In that clouded state we fantasized a whole host of things. We assented to the prevailing idea that "any change is for the better." It never dawned on us that we do not invent anything new. We merely discover something that is already there. Nature eventually gives up its secrets ever so slowly.

Sociology has a term for this blue skying activity. Wishful thinking in which progress precedes an acceptable norm is known as cultural lag. Even products we have used for years suddenly bear such labels as "new and improved" or "as seen on TV." Many reject "today" for a return to "yesterday." There is security in doing something like we always have, that is, the old fashioned way or simply handmade. Some groups even withdraw completely and self-segregate. The Amish are perhaps the best examples of this withdrawal.

When it comes to motivation, psychologists hold that the majority of people do not act on what they know, but how they feel. Attitudes are more motivational than knowledge. We all know the speed limit but freely exceed it and risk the consequences of a ticket. Our prisons are filled with non-complaint individuals. Change can not only occur rapidly but also in many instances unperceptively.

Let's visit a small, homogeneous city of 2,000 a mere forty years ago. In this middle-western city, 4,000 eyes scrutinized the actions of each resident. Young people were special targets. One's good reputation was a major concern of mostly everyone. "What will the neighbors think?" Morality was strict. No premarital or extramarital sex was a moral code everyone consented to. Entertainment for young people consisted of a movie theatre and a heavily chaperoned canteen on the weekend.

A 10:00 p.m. curfew was in effect seven days a week. A siren sounded every night at exactly 10:00 p.m. All young people needed to either be at home or with an adult. Consequently, the police did not have much to do. City ordinances were a self-enforced affair.

Sexual activity was limited to those who were married. Even condoms were a sort of prescription item. They were discreetly behind counters and had to be requested. Only adult, married individuals could request them.

Somehow in this strict, adult environment, Bob managed to get Sally pregnant. Marriage was the only option. No one expected this to happen. This was a new experience for which they had no "punishment." The young couple sought to make the necessary arrangements with their religious leader. To their dismay, he refused to witness their wedding! The baby had to have a name! To marry them would be a sign of approval for their obvious promiscuity. The local justice of the peace agreed. It would amount to approval.

Seeking the blessings of marriage, the young couple went to the neighboring city fifteen miles away. The response was the same: marriage would mean approval. It was an infraction of the prevailing moral code. The girl was expelled from high school but the young man was permitted to continue his education. One last effort to secure a marriage took them to the "big city" fifty-three miles away. There they received a civil ceremony. Their troubles were only just beginning!

As a newly married couple, they returned home. To their surprise, no one would rent to them. Again the idea of approval was the major issue. Finally in desperation, the young couple purchased a mobile home. However, the local trailer court refused to allow them to rent a space. As a last resort, the boy's father allowed them to put their mobile home in his front yard. But wait, this is not the end of the story! The father was the manager of the one of the largest businesses in town. The board of directors met and served notice in view of his son's public scandal which could affect their business; he was given a thirty-day notice and terminated.

Have our attitudes about sex and sexual activity of young people changed in the past years? Are there any social sanctions against what we at one time publicly called immorality? Are pregnant girls permitted to continue their education? Sociology calls a lack of norms for any activity an anomaly. A divorce was also next to impossible to obtain. One couple came close but ultimately had to give up their "immoral" decision. By the way, this city was the county seat of one of the state's largest counties!

Ted Howard's book, *Who Should Play God* should be a required reading for every teacher. Although the book bears a 1977 copyright, many of his predictions for the future are the current mores today. Is this a confirmation of "any change is for the better!"

Let's look at this sex example once again. A mere twenty-five years ago, Joshua Lederberg listed eight responses to the question, "Where do babies come from?" Bob and Sally had only one choice: the simple old fashioned intercourse!

1. Artificial insemination of a wife by her husband.
2. Artificial insemination by a donor.
3. Ovarian, or egg, transplant from one woman to another and subsequent artificial insemination by either the husband or a selected donor.
4. Fertilization of an egg in vitro.
5. Extracorporeal gestation (test tube baby).
6. Parthenogenesis (virgin birth).
7. Nuclear transplantation or cloning, in which a cell is made to produce an exact genetic duplicate of the donor of the nucleus, male or female.
8. Embryo fusion, or the joining together of the two individual embryos to form a human with four biological parents instead of the traditional two.

When or how did any of the above become possible or even moral? Some religions call any of these "clinically adultery."

Why is this discussion about sex important? What relevance does any of this have to the future? The mores (morals) of a mere fifty years ago have greatly changed. Condoms are openly sold in a variety of stores. Colleges and some high schools give them away at no cost to students. A former Surgeon General of the United States admonished states to adopt free condoms merely for the asking!

A major discussion today centers around "what is human?" What are the acceptable limits or boundaries on human experimentation? Are some individuals more important than others? What is the modern application of "greater love has no man than he lays his life down for a friend?" As we all know, the possible soon becomes the expected! If it is immoral to sell a human being, is it moral to sell the components of what will eventually make a human being?

Human engineering has become one of the major enterprises in today's world. Dr. James Cameron, a local geneticist, assembled thirty religious leaders for moral guidance for his work. Thirty days later he dismissed them because they basically could not agree or provide any credible guidance to a person Dr. Cameron had who was seeking his personal identity. "Won't you at least show me the syringe that you used?"

If one of the major roles of the teaching profession is to pass on a culture's value, what comprises today's curriculum? Many groups complain or even forbid any instruction involving values of any kind. Is this one of the reasons why the largest school district in the country today is homeschooling?

MIT premiered a new experiment that few would have any moral objections to. Fortunately for us, it was displayed on the 60-minute program on April 22, 2018. It can be accessed online and is certainly worth viewing. It gives a whole new meaning to the command most of us heard, "mind me!" Through an ingenious invention one's thoughts can be transferred to a computer. Thoughts sent to one's vocal cords are intercepted before they are spoken. The apparatus can be attached to the head and dreams can be recorded.

The subject on camera ordered a pizza with his thoughts. What he ordered was actually delivered. Think of what this will mean for those who have lost the ability to speak! By the same token, the human mind had access to the contents of all the information "online." Is this a modern day example of HAL In the motion picture, "*A Space Odyssey?*"

Years ago, Scott French combined the writing styles and attributes of established authors. The result was the book, *Just This Once*. Imagine a book produced by a computer. Let's leave the subject of computers for a moment. Most of us know the power and influence of all sorts of media. Let's look at "food."

The Archer Daniels Midland Company based in Kansas City demonstrated some new achievements in the area of food. This company is famous for its wheat deals with Red China. They gave the audience food that was devoid of any calories. Little if any difference in taste. They also distributed dry water! Yes, dry water! Paper bags filled with water! How? Drops of water were encased in dissolvable capsules.

Milk in numerous flavors that will never spoil. It needs no refrigeration. Think of those areas in the world that have no electricity. This merely is the tip of the iceberg. The Greek philosopher, Heraclitus, wrote that "change" is the only constant. We change our minds, change our clothes, now we can invent the future through change.

Thirty years ago, a social scientist predicted that eventually there would be only two symphony orchestras in the United States. One would be on the east coast and the other on the west coast. Both unfortunately would be in a museum. This seems almost impossible. However, during the rehearsal break of the Minnesota Symphony, the second violinist admonished us NOT to attend their concerts. "We actually sound so much better on our recordings."

By a coincidence, that orchestra endured a whole year of a lockout. However, their recordings were a national best seller. Their CDs are labeled "High Fidelity." Perhaps they should carry the mark, "Higher Fidelity." How would Mozart and Beethoven respond to this sound technology? While on the subject of music, note the physical effect of the 60 beat a minute music that some schools use in the learning process with fantastic results. This type of music is also used in prenatal care with positive results. Hospitals use it to prep patients for surgery.

In the 1970s, Harper and Row produced a series of outstanding and controversial film strips that dealt with cultural lag. They are still available in many college media centers. One of the film strips deals with the sewing of an old rat to a young rat. Sharing so many physical functions had a marked positive effect on the older rat. Should this experiment be transferred to humans? If so, what would be an acceptable procedure to accomplish this? The series raises the important question, "Does space travel require some human adjustments in an environment inimical to human life?"

Selective amnesia is most likely only words on paper. We often say, "Just don't give it a thought," or "Just forget about it." Is it possible to erase some memories that hinder our well-being? Let's explore this phenomenon. We have all had unmotivated students at one time or another who have no intention of passing our class. "Joe" enrolled in sociology. He was grossly overweight; always wore sunglasses. The teacher never knew if his eyes were open or shut. He responded to an occasional question with a simple grunt.

True to form, he never completed a single assignment. The teacher had no alternative but to "write him off." Class time needed to be given to those who cared. The president of the American College of Hypnotists came as a guest speaker. He shared among other examples how he erased some traumatic feelings from some of his patients. Under hypnotic trance he put a kind of band aid on the memory that caused such pain. Joe was awake despite his sun glasses.

As the teacher approached his office one morning, Joe was waiting outside his door. He raised the teacher off of the floor while shouting, "Give me the phone number of that doctor or I will kill you!" He had been sleeping with a woman twice his age and mistook it for love until she threw him out. Joe needed to forget her, hence, the need for the doctor. The teacher phoned the doctor to tell him what to expect. "Not to worry, I can handle this." Joe remained in my memory as the ugliest, most disliked, ever. Joe never returned to class. The teacher felt relieved! But it doesn't end here.

Several years later when the school day was over, the teacher was making his way to the teacher's parking lot. A young man greeted him with "Hello Mr. Poplau." He was slim, smile in his voice, sported a navy uniform, and no sun glasses. "I'm sorry, I don't know you." "This is "Joe."

The transformation was unbelievable. The teacher could not resist asking, "How is "Jane" doing?" "Jane who?" He had no recollection of the woman who caused him so much trauma years ago. He also had no recollection of the threat on the teacher's life.

Process this. Should this be an option for our crowded prisons? Read the book, *A Clockwork Orange* or better yet, view the motion picture. Some critics consider it to be the finest motion picture of the 20th century. The minister of the interior in London, performed a new method, The Ludovico Technique. It is similar to aversion treatment. The author, Burgess, disapproved of the behaviorism of B.F. Skinner. By means of this new method of conditioning, the subject, Alex, becomes the "perfect Christian." He has lost his free will. He is good, but not of his choosing. Is virtue only in the choosing?

Because of the controversy, Stanley Kubrick removed the film from Great Britain for twenty-seven years. Kubrick omitted the book's final chapter but presents the redemption of a teenage delinquent by condition-reflex. Should this method of rehabilitation be considered? The United States now has more people in prison than some countries have people. Seventy-five percent of ex-convicts return to prison. They are once again guilty of an anti-social act. Is it effective? "Joe" is now enjoying a completely new and happy life. More on prisons and their effectiveness in the final chapters of this book.

Once again, the future is not merely the production of new or different products. It consists of new attitudes "The same old, same old" is no longer effective in a dynamic society such as ours. MIT is searching for students with the most bizarre ideas. By instilling skills in our students, they will produce a future we will never see. Man made footprints on the moon, because a teacher made marks on his brain. Maybe we even erased some unpleasant marks! One thing for sure: we will never lose our need for one another. The Africans got it right: UBUNTO, "I am because you are!" That can never be erased under any conditions!

Chapter 12

A Community Service Class
The Philosophical Basis

"Nothing but what you volunteer has the essence of life, the springs of pleasure in it. These are the things you do because you want to do them, the things that your spirit has chosen for its satisfaction."

—Woodrow Wilson

You are a transfer student to Shawnee Mission Northwest High School. Your yellow enrollment form indicates your next class will be community service. This was really not by first choice but no other class was available. Christmas music fills the room. Decorated Christmas trees are in every available space. How can this be? It's August! The holidays are in three months! You silently remind yourself that you have two days to change your schedule.

The instructor appears to be pleasant. He begins the class with three questions that puzzles him:

1. If you don't eat food for a month, what will happen?
2. If you do not drink any liquids for at least a month, what happens?
3. If you do not do any community service, you most assuredly are going to die. It will be a most painful death!

This can't possibly be true. This has to be the way the teacher overstates the importance of his class. He sounds like he means it. Why the Christmas music and the Christmas trees? The holidays are three months away. He better be convincing or I'm dropping this class for sure!

THE RENE SPITZ STUDY

Although born in Vienna in 1887 in a wealthy Jewish family, he spent most of his childhood in Hungary. Earning a degree in psychology, he applied the teachings of Freud to children. This was something new. However, anti-Jewish attitudes force Spitz to flee to France. For safety he eventually immigrated to the United States. The university welcomed him as a staff person. There he began his most famous study which ultimately became the basis for Northwest's community service class. He assembled a competent staff. Many of them were medical nurses.

Their instructions were simple and direct: find as many orphaned babies and bring them to my laboratory. The younger the better, certainly no toddlers. In a short time, his staff brought fifty-five babies only to hear his strange directions. Each baby was to get his/her own crib. When they are hungry, feed them. When they are cold, cover them up or adjust the temperature. When they are wet, change them. Under no circumstances do you pick them up or hug them. Do not even speak to them at any time.

Spitz brought in a movie crew and sporadically photographed the babies and the activities of the staff. In less than a month's time, it became obvious that something was radically wrong with those babies. They began to tremble and shake uncontrollably. Staff members found it difficult not to pick them up. In fact, many staff members quit citing child abuse and inhumane treatment. At the conclusion of one year, twenty-seven babies were found dead in their cribs.

Seven more died in the second year. Eventually, the remaining twenty-one also succumbed. On the death certificates, Spitz wrote a very strange word for the cause of death: marasmus. The word which is Greek, means to die from a lack of affection. Some authorities held their deaths were due to child abuse, sensory deprivation, they were all sick to begin with! We would all agree that those babies were not given the opportunity to bond to anyone. Spitz coined a new word, anaclitic depression. Anaclitic is simply defined as "without anyone to lean on."

Humans must rely on others to "lean on" or they die. Spitz eventually performed this study in South America with one thousand babies. Without the human touch or involvement, death results.

Whatever our origin: God, evolution, processes of nature, the final "person" is born incomplete. We complete ourselves through the service of others. Humans are born devoid of any survival instincts. Aristotle called the mind a tabula raza or blank table. What animals do by instinct, humans must do by reason. It is the socialization process whereby we become human. Through the actions of others, we learn to speak, what is edible; absorb our culture with its values and mores.

Fortunately the film Spitz produced of his experiment is available online. A warning: it will depress you almost permanently. Some comments made by viewers online:

"So so sad, I wanted to reach through the screen and pick him up and hug him!"
"God have mercy!"
"Screw science!"
"This is almost too tough to watch—heartbreaking"

Every living adolescent or adult has experienced love at some time in infancy. Love is the greatest service we can give. Victor Hugo said it best: "The supreme happiness in life is the conviction that we loved!"

A Northwest student left school after his third hour class. He chose a secluded spot by a nearby lake. There he proceeded to cut his wrists in an attempt to kill himself. With wrists still bleeding he returned to school. In tears he told a teacher: "I'm very plain. My mother and father are divorced. My mother lives in another state. When I come home, my father has just left for work. When he comes home, I have gone to school. There has to be something more than this. I feel no one loves me."

Only after psychiatric care was he able to feel somewhat loved. In a very real sense, our lives belong to someone else. Scripture emphatically states that our eternal salvation rests upon how we treat others as ourselves.

BRUNO BETTELHEIM

Millions of normal, well-adjusted people were exterminated in the holocaust. Someone had to give the order to murder them simply because they were of the Jewish faith. Is it true that once human, always human? Can we in fact lose our humanness? No one would deny that normal individuals do not kill in that magnitude. Adolph Eichmann grew up as a religious person. He and his mother read the scriptures every day. As an adolescent and young adult he was well liked. In 1942 he became the famous "desk killer" sending millions to their death. Eventually he fled to Argentina. Despite his past, he didn't even need sleeping pills! He ceased to be a human being.

Dr. Bruno Bettelheim, born in Vienna in 1903, spent a year in a Nazi concentration camp. After gaining his freedom he immigrated to the United States. He began to study disturbed children at the University of Chicago. One of his specialties was feral children. In reality, his studies were an extension of the Rene Spitz study. Without the benefit of community service, children reverted to the animal stage. They never spoke, preferred raw meat and prowled around at night in their cages.

His account of this phenomenon he described at great length in his book, *The Informed Heart.* Many of his conclusions were entered as evidence in the trial of Eichmann. When we cease all forms of community service, marasmus results. The mission statement of the Northwest community service class is just six words: THE DOER OF GOOD BECOMES GOOD!

Several times each semester, only the lights from the Christmas trees lighten the room. Soft Christmas carols provide a humane background. Students even bring some of their favorite Christmas albums. One young man was overheard saying, "I just love to come into this room!"

After viewing much of the Rene Spitz video, students are appalled at the effect we have on others. Columbine now takes on a new understanding. We are our brother's keeper. Our first guest speakers are a middle aged couple who define what it means to be poor and needy. Cases of canned food line the back of the room. Bags of clothing are by the Christmas trees. Students learn very quickly that their worst day is someone's best day.

The transfer student decided to remain in the class. She enrolled again the second semester. On the final day of the school year, with tears in her eyes, she hugged the teacher. With all the emotion and conviction she said, "Merry Christmas." It's like hearing "joy to the world for the very first time."

Chapter 13

The Mechanics of a Community Service Class

A journey of any length begins with a proverbial first step. The service class will gradually evoke and take on some personal characteristics of its own. Initially, Northwest scheduled its one class during the final hour of the school day. By this arrangement, enrolled students would not have to miss any of their other classes. Seventeen students of every ability piloted the first semester offering. By the second semester, the enrollment had grown to twice that number. Some students had to be turned away.

The class was added to the social science department. In another district school, the nurse directed the service class. You might be asking, what will the students do on a daily basis? The enrollment eventually soared to 480. The sponsor was relieved of any supervision to accommodate the growing numbers. For the sake of clarity, here are the mechanics in an outline form.

1. The class is limited to juniors and seniors. Student must provide their own transportation.
2. The sponsor needs to contact all the neighboring schools to obtain elementary and middle school teachers who will accept a student aid on a daily basis. Each school will have a teacher who will take the responsibility to oversee the program in their school. This does not constitute a major increase in their work load. It is more procedural than substantive.
3. Students are absolutely honored to return as a teacher's aide in their previous elementary or middle school. Likewise, teachers are excited to have some of their students return to assist them. It was not uncommon to send twenty students each hour to a single school.
4. Teachers assign them to a variety of projects: correct papers, make copies, private tutor, especially in math, lead discussions, assist in the library, help

in gym classes or recess. One teacher remarked, "It is like having another teacher in the room!"

5. The school office has a sign-in and sign-out page for whatever hour the students are there to give assistance.
6. Retirement homes provide numerous opportunities: visiting residents, assisting at scheduled games, writing or reading letters, delivering mail to the residents. One student said, "This is like having the grandparent I never had!"
7. Some special education teachers at the high school provide opportunities for student involvement.
8. For variety, some students serve at various sites during the week: schools, retirement homes, thrift stores, community centers.

Trust is the key to a successful community service program. In fact, trust is an important part of the lives of each one of us. A level of trust is so essential to our lives that we do not appreciate it until it is gone. We trust the people who have processed and shipped our food have done so conscientiously. We trust the safety of our cars at 70 miles per hour and a jet airplane at 800 miles per hour. But there is a tendency to withhold trust at the educational level.

A college professor had a unique way of demonstrating trust. The grade in his class depended on a single exam, given at the end of the semester. The class was very intense. The instructor, after distributing the exam, turned his back on the class. He began reading a book. Given every opportunity, no one cheated!

We expect perfection from our adolescents. We never expect perfection from fellow adults. The element of control in schools is second only to control in prisons. There is a need for procedural trust, but one could question the extensive checking of permission slips that borders on active mistrust. Trust is a value that can only be learned by doing. On day one, students in a community service class must be given an element of complete trust. They lose it only if they abuse it. When trust slowly becomes a habit, reliability results and a changed individual is produced.

The consequences of truancy, even once, no matter when it occurs, even on the final day, that student is terminated from the class with all loss of credit. Truancy is defined as checking out but not showing up at his/her site. It is a joy to see how assiduous students are in being trustworthy. The number of students dropped from the class is almost negligible!

Special events result from invitations from the community: school carnivals, community dinners, job Olympics, a weekend prom for senior citizens. Students actually dated senior citizens plus had a limousine to take them for ride! Many students said that experience was even better than their own junior/senior prom!

CODE SIX FORMS

We all know there are some classes or class days that are less important than others. Some teachers give the students a "free hour" a month. Code Six forms, signed by parents, and each class the students will miss, allows the students to miss either that single hour or an entire day for approved community activities, for example, supervising job Olympics. This form bears a resemblance to those used for field trips. Students are limited to two of them a month.

GRADES

All classes require some form of evaluation. Grades are set up on the basis of time. A student can have only five excused absences without a penalty. These five consist of other field trips or activities in other classes. After five absences, the student must make up one hour for each hour missed. All grades are figured by the quarter. Incidentally, the most common grade is a well-deserved A.

The CCC at Northwest is a semester offering. The total number of hours is divided in half for the semester grade. If the student has twenty hours the first quarter and forty hours the second quarter, it will result in an A for the semester average. Grades are distributed as follows:

A. Thirty hours beyond the class time.
B. Fifteen hours beyond the class time.
C. Ten hours beyond the class time.
D. Three hours beyond the class time.
E. No hours beyond the class time.

THE EXECUTIVE BOARD

The executive board has genuine power. It possesses the power to overrule the class sponsor. The executive board decides which projects the class will undertake. The class must have a constitution conceived by the executive board. Individuals become members of the board by submitting an essay to the current president and vice president, who in turn choose the students they feels will best serve the CCC. In most instances, the sponsor chooses the president. The president, in turn, chooses the vice president. There is an interview process.

The board will meet periodically or when there is a major decision that must be made. Some of the projects include

1. A dinner to raise money for the medical needs of a three-year-old boy. This netted a profit of 22,000 dollars. The students used the school cafeteria and kitchen and all the food was donated by local grocery stores.
2. Participation in a bone marrow match screening to find a match for a 12-year-old boy and a senior boy who would die without it. Hundreds of students and adults from the community were type-matched and a match was found for the 12-year-old boy. He is currently doing very well.
3. Garage sales are held twice a year. Each sale usually nets about 2,000 dollars. Whatever isn't sold is donated to the community thrift store.
4. Monthly generational dances are held at the school with about two hundred area senior citizens attending. The dances are held on a Saturday evenings with dinner and dessert prepared and served by the students.
5. Faculty appreciation parties are held monthly.
6. A yearly pancake feast is sponsored by local optimists club with the profits used for two CCC scholarships.
7. Tutoring for delinquent boys at Associated Youth Services occurs twice a week.
8. Assisting in a local thrift store. All profits go to the poor and needy.
9. Painting a house of a man who had suffered a heart attack. The students did it all in just under three hours.
10. Holding book drives for an inner city grade school.

Kansas State Representative, Lisa Benlon, introduced a bill that would require every Kansas High School to offer community service in their daily curriculum. CCC students lobbied for its passage. They were both eloquent and passionate in the state legislature in Topeka, Kansas. A sample of their presentation:

> "When I imagine my future, I do not think of trigonometry, or chemistry, or of Shakespearean sonnets. I think of what I will always remember from my days at Shawnee Mission Northwest High School. This knowledge, I did not gain in a computer lab or after-school practice session, or really even a classroom. I stand before you today and can honestly say that I had a chance to truly learn about people, and the real world outside Johnson County through Cougars Community Commitment classes."

Too often in the daily lives of teenagers, one gets bogged down with monotony and day-to-day stress. The CCC program allows students not only the chance to give back to the community, but to develop as a whole person and build character. My personal commitment to the CCC is what I am the most proud of.

I have worked extremely hard pushing myself academically for the past four years to maintain a 4.0 GPA. This pales in comparison to all the children that I've helped to learn their spelling words of the week and the large smiles and hugs I've received after they earn their first 100 percent paper. CCC has opened my heart and my mind, and it has done much the same for hundreds of students before me. This class is a necessity. As our motto states: THE DOER OF GOOD BECOMES GOOD."

House bill 2352 passed overwhelmingly and went into effect on July 2002. More than a quarter of a century later, Community Service Enrollment at Shawnee Mission Northwest is sky.

Chapter 14

A Case Study

Heather

It is service that dignifies, and only service.

—Woodrow Wilson

Finally the day came for the first CCC class of the school year. The administrator in charge of enrollment promised to "fill it up with late enrollees and transfer students." The sponsor's expectations were high on that first day in August 1992. To his dismay, only four students comprised the community service class. In that first class was a senior girl with a very questionable background. With her background, there is no way she could ever be successful in a class that would be based on trust.

To all appearances, the teacher had made a monumental mistake. The girl in question had already dropped out of school but agreed to return and attempt to finish her high school education. She had been a problem student ever since her parents divorced when she was in the sixth grade. Name the drug and she took it. Chances were she was on something that very moment. The mother confided that her drug habit was so bad, she would set the alarm for every two hours. If Heather was in her bed, fine. If not, the mother would go out looking for her hoping to find her alive.

She froze with every ring of the phone: is it the police? Have they found her either dead or overdosed with her fellow druggies?

The teacher's dream of a special class was dashed! The four students would have to see their counselors for some other class. Heather straightened up and rubbed her nose like being hit by a foul odor. "Give me until Thursday to see if I can get enough students to have this class." What kind of students would she recruit? Drug addicts? Attendance problems? Was it even worth the gamble?

On Thursday the teacher walked in to a class of seventeen students! Heather said with a sense of personal triumph, "Are these enough to have the class?" Her eyes locked on the teacher's for what seemed like an eternity. She was searching the depths of his soul. Heather exhibited a keen desire for acceptance and approval.

The teacher suddenly felt a kindred spirit and a "second chance." The silence was deafening. He had bet against this class on the very first day. There would never be a class like this. They would meet only to disperse somewhere in the community. Could this group be trusted? Was it even worth a try? Over his whole teaching career, the teacher had always regarded himself as a student advocate. That positive attitude was about to be trusted! Did he dare allow them an autonomous role in the community? Do people really have the capacity to change?

Sitting in front of him were seventeen young people recruited by an acknowledged "problem" student. What did she promise them? Would the opportunity to begin a whole new approach to education be lost? These were decisions of monumental importance and they needed to be made instantly. Smiling, the instructor took a leap of faith and said, "Welcome! This will be the class of your life!" Heather became the acknowledged president of the class.

To digress for a moment, Heather, like so many other students, was exposed to the philosophy of "read and recite, tell and test, or sit and get." She had never been trusted. Success eluded her. Now her leadership potential surfaced for the first time in her education career. She and the other sixteen students were now in charge of their own education. She even came up with the name for the class: COUGARS COMMUNITY COMMITMENT or simply The CCC. She formed committees, found projects to do. The teacher's dream was beginning to materialize! She discovered that her worst day was someone else's best day!

Heather's grades in all of her classes began to rise. For the first time in her life, she was on the honor roll. Heather began to give things away from home. "I almost had to tie the refrigerator down. Heather wanted to give it away! How could I say no, I was finally getting my daughter back," her mother said. "I had been praying for this moment!" Her attendance was almost perfect. Most importantly, her drug use ceased. To the amazement of everyone, here was a young lady from an above-average home who would sit on dirty floors, fight off cockroaches and spend hours with numerous less fortunate families.

People now mattered more to her than anything else. Under her leadership, she found the 40,000 dollars a family needed to save their home. She found plumbers, electricians. She even chose between attending her prom and giving a crucial speaking engagement. It took her only seconds to choose the speaking engagement. In the audience was her mother beaming with pride!

Heather's example drew awards from Noxzema, Prudential, Optimists, Kiwanis, and Sertoma. The *Kansas City Star* did a four-page article on the CCC as an example of compassion. At the end of the first year, the class was nominated for Penney's Golden Rule Award. The evening of the presentation brought the school principal, Heather, Heather's mother, and the sponsor. The competition was keen. When the CCC was chosen for the first prize, the sponsor said to Heather, "You go up with the principal, it's your award!" Heather rose, shoulders back, acknowledged the standing ovation. Her mother was in tears at her daughter's transformation.

Shortly after, with graduation only a month away, students signed up to be potential speakers at the graduation ceremony. To the surprise of many, Heather was first on the sign-up sheet. She was chosen from the long list of potential speakers. On graduation night, Heather rose to address the crowd of thousands. Before she began her prepared speech, she looked at her mother and said, "Mom, I love you!" Her sheer excellence mesmerized the packed house. Her metamorphosis was complete. The doer of good had become good.

That night as the sponsor prepared for bed, he thanked God for the class that had changed Heather and so many others. Heather had learned what you do for others comes back a hundredfold. As Heather's mother and stepfather prepared for bed, that graduation night, a unique exhaustion and euphoria came over her mother. Just before turning out the lights, the stepfather noticed that his wife was already asleep, but the alarm clock was not set for the usual two-hour check. It would never be set that way again.

Heather went on to college. But her story does not end here. Prior to the first Christmas since her graduation, her parents made an appointment with the sponsor of the CCC at Northwest. In the faculty lounge, they laid down eight one hundred dollar bills. They choked out, "This is what we would have spent on Christmas. Our Christmas is having out daughter back!" The mother choked out, "This was a class from God." The next Christmas they donated 1,000 dollars.

Gradually, enrollment included nearly every identified problem students in school. "If the program could change Heather, then it can change anyone." A judge over one hundred miles away put a delinquent into the program. Local probation officers did likewise. The vice-principal in charge of student discipline privately told the sponsor to keep this particular student out of school as much as you can. Your class seems to be the only class he likes. His classmates had officially requested that student be removed from school or at least in their classes.

He enrolled in the CCC for an entire year. He is now a medic, a first responder. He frequently emails his experiences. Virtue is its own reward.

There are almost countless numbers of personal transformations. One student bonded with an elderly man who unfortunately died during the school year. The student gave his eulogy at the funeral! Another student stopped the sponsor in the hallway. In a broken voice admitted, "I only took your class to get out of school. I no longer feel that way!" Frequently CCC students would request the teacher to report them absent for that day. The reason. They were coming only for their CCC hour.

In appreciation for the class efforts on behalf of the city of Shawnee, the mayor presented the keys to the city to the class sponsor. As a bonus, he dedicated an entire day to the CCC! In the words of sacred scripture, "Strength was made perfect in infirmity." Maybe Heather's mother was correct, this is a class from God!

Chapter 15

Bells and Cells

Let's pretend for a moment that God suddenly decided to install an answering machine in heaven. The experience would go something like this:

Thank you for calling heaven.
For English, press one.
For Spanish, press two.
For all other languages, press three.
Please select one of the following options:
Press one for request.
Press two for thanksgiving.
Press three for complaints.
Press four for all others.

I am sorry, all our angels and saints are busy helping other sinners right now. However, your prayer is important to us and we will answer it in the order it was received. Please stay on the line. If you would like to speak to:

God, press one
Jesus, press two
Holy Spirit, press three

To find a loved one who has been assigned to heaven press five, and then enter his social security number followed by the pound sign.

If you receive a negative response, please hang up and dial area code 666. For reservations to heaven, enter JOHN followed by the numbers, 316.

Our computers show that you have already been prayed for today, please hang up and call again tomorrow.

The office is now closed for the weekend to observe a religious holiday. If you are calling after hours and need emergency assistance, please contact your local pastor. Thank you and have a heavenly day!

Absurd! Some may call this example sacrilegious. God does not speak to our ears but to our hearts. This far-fetched example is meant to illustrate the current movement to rely more and more on technology. Places of worship sport ATM machines for worshippers' convenience. With drive through mortuaries we can view loved ones from the privacy of our cars! Life as we know it is changing quickly and substantially. An important question: are we substituting convenience for humaneness?

Are you lonesome? Short of friends? Subscribe to dial a friend. You can enjoy a personal call when and how often you need a personal conversation. Be sure to pay your monthly bill by a credit card, check, or cash! Need a prescription renewed? Simply call the pharmacy. It can either be mailed to you or simply "drive through" and pick it up. Ask yourself: do these conveniences produce a "freedom from" or a "freedom for?"

There are a plethora of studies that document the effects of isolation on human beings. We don't have to take anyone's word for it, we can watch the effects on technology in vivid living color. How is this possible?

Let's turn our attention to American prisons. Currently we have the distinction of having more people behind bars than any other country on earth. The guiding philosophy before the 1970s was rehabilitation. Many prisons employed a work release program in which those incarcerated could actually be paid a minimum wage. Upon their release they had a sufficient amount of money for the basic necessities to begin life over again. With the emphasis on punishment, all this changed after the 70s. This produced drastic results.

Henry Floyd Brown had the unique distinction of being one of the longest serving convicts in American history. He escaped the death penalty to experience fifty-four years in nine different prisons. Those years included multiple periods in solitary confinement. That meant he had no human interaction whatsoever. The Kansas Secretary of Correction considered Henry to be the most dangerous and cunning criminal ever to occupy a cell in the 110 years history of the Kansas State Prison.

The author had known Henry for several years prior to his release. He received the following letter as he contemplated his parole:

Now that I am really close to getting out . . . it is a scary feeling to see myself walking out like the day I was born except now, no one will be there to take care of me until I learn to walk . . . I want to be a productive member of society. Will they help me? . . . no gifts, just a job where I can earn my way at a living wage. I have nothing. I am worse off than a refugee who floats up out of the sea. There are program and loans to help the refugee, but there are no programs to help the ex-con. No doubt I can get food stamps, but where will I cook the food? In the past, I just robbed something . . . but I have no intention of doing that this time . . . ask one of your classes. Maybe they will have some ideas. Love and peace, Kansas State Prison

Like so many other prisons, The Kansas State Prison has reached its capacity. To put a new person behind the walls, someone has to be released. Well might prisons be regarded as a sort of microcosm of our society. Many—too many—believe that "times have changed." The Renee Spitz study is no longer current. Another relevant study that comes to almost the same conclusion: human beings need social interaction to remain human. Sheldon and Eleanor Glueck spent their entire professional lives on the causes of American criminality. They identified certain types that produce anti-social behavior. They identified them with strange terminology:

1. The endomorph: laid back, easy going. When frustrated, he/she seeks to be with other people.
2. The ectomorph: the quiet, sensitive type. When frustrated, he merely wants to be alone. "Get out of my face!"
3. The mesomorph: the outgoing individual, when frustrated, he/she wants to fight back. "Let's organize."

The mesomorph excels in almost every kind of anti-social behavior: alcohol abuse, drugs, violence. His/her appearance is physically above average, for example, Pretty Boy Floyd. "Lock 'em up and throw away the key" philosophy will have little or no effect on this type of person. Teachers: check out the school's detention room. You will find a predominance of this type of personality. The behavior has to be channeled into something meaningful such as community service.

An example of what not to do consisted of having the offending students write the Declaration of Independence backward. To add to this assignment, the teacher counted every word! The result was predicable: The frustrated (mesomorph) student keyed the teacher's new car. The final interview the Gluecks gave to the media emphasized the absolute need for the human touch! They also concluded that today's young people are in effect raising themselves. Without the application of love, they predicted a wave of violence that will sweep the country.

Who could deny the lengthy study done by Victoria Secunda. Her conclusion stated simply was those young people turned out to be the best where there is a lot of adult involvement in their lives—another example of the effect of social interaction. The community service students (CCC) have a minimum of one hour a day of adult supervision. Few if any are in the school's detention room. Channel, not punishment.

One can see and even experience the social isolationism prevalent in our prisons. The author was a counselor for eleven years at the Kansas Correctional Institution. Like many prisons we inaugurated the Scared Straight Program. Our initial group was composed of three young boys. Our intention was simply to introduce them to the horrors of prison life. Our final activity took us to solitary confinement. This was a new experience for the author.

Rarely are visitors permitted in that area. The experience was nothing short of terrifying! Inmates were screaming and threw human waste at our small group. One of the young men was enticed to a cell. By tugging at his shirt, his life was saved. Had he been an arm's length from the cell he would have been crushed to death! All of the cell occupants were at one time normal. Social isolation reduced them to "feral animals."

With the assistance of your computer, you can experience the effects of solitary confinement. The State of Maine permitted a film crew to photograph its solitary confinement over a three-year period. A warning before you opt to see this film: it is not only violent but very disturbing. This is the daily environment for over 80,000 Americans—key in *Last Days of Solitary*.

The Pelican Bay State Prison in California holds the distinction of being one of the toughest prisons in the United States. Dr. Craig Haney conducted interviews of all those serving time in solitary confinement. Most of them had never been outside their windowless, concrete cells. He returned twenty years later and found many of the men still there. Some had requested the death penalty. Haney called it "social death." Fifty percent of all prison suicides occur in solitary confinement. This is not an example of "one apple" spoiling the rest. It is the barrel itself that is the source of the corruption!

What is needed is a creative solution to address and alleviate this condition. These conditions are not new. Read *"The Devil's Front Porch,"* written in 1970 by L.D. Johnson, an inmate at the Kansas prison. Dr. Philip Zimbardo's, *"The Lucifer Effect,"* is an absolute classic on the ultimate effect of social isolation. His famous experiment at Stanford has now been made into a Hollywood film.

No doubt many of you might be saying, "So what, they had it coming. They made their bed now let them lie in it!" In actual reality, most convicts are eventually released including those in solitary confinement. At least 75 percent of them will return to prison. In order to return, they must once again commit some anti-social behaviors: theft, rape and murder, comprise the most common offenses.

To illustrate what has been termed, a life sentence, on the installment plan occurred shortly after a much sought after release. Unfortunately, the parolee had no job, the 100 dollar gate money went for food; he sought shelter in a homeless shelter for one month. In desperation he walked back to the prison, some twenty-six miles away, and asked the warden to be readmitted.

The response was simple, "We can't take you back unless you commit another crime." Consequently, he went to the nearest gas station, held it up, went out to the curb, sat down and waited for the police. He died in prison some years later. Alone, without friends or family, he was buried in the prison's potter's field.

What can we do to change this? It is mandatory that we commence our quest for change with a new guiding philosophy. Our long-range objective for these offenders is a return to a normal state. Certainly that is not happening under the current system. Ramsey Clark stated that we can judge the quality of a society by the way it treats those who offend it. There are signs of hope.

The Kansas penal system began a program whereby thirty men went by bus to a local factory. Part of their salary paid for their upkeeping at the prison. Most of it was held by the prison to give to the inmates on the day they were released. It was not unusual on the release day to be given 15,000 dollars. That meant he could afford housing, a car, secure a job, plus he had work skills. No one outside the prison makes license plates!

We hear so much about the trade inequity especially with China. Why not establish factories in prison to make and sell many of the items we import from the Far East? A cursory glance in any American store, especially Walmart, has the *Made in China* sticker on it. Prisoners would be delighted to make those products. They would have worker/product identification. Imagine how this would affect their self-image—not to mention their pocketbooks.

Unfortunately, some prison residents choose not to work. Currently, the prison cafeteria has become the most violent area in the prison. How can we creatively change this? By making the cafeteria resemble a McDonalds, a Wendy's, Burger King. Convicts would be able to choose their meal. The cost would be deducted from their account. It was Napoleon who stated, "An army travels on its stomach!" Using that philosophy, it would not take long to achieve full employment. "Choice" is a basic human attribute.

Ultimately the men and women would be paroled with not only sufficient cash, but possess work skills as well. These are skills and choices they will continue when they re-enter society. Is this new approach achievable? We can begin by reversing our current prison philosophy from punishment to rehabilitation.

The average prisoner spends about three years behind bars. The author has heard the gut-wrenching cries of convicts, especially during the holidays. Many of those in the "bells and cells" at one time were seated in our class-room. Dr. Spock was asked why he was demonstrating—how did this have any relevance to being a baby authority? His response: "I care about the type of society those babies will grow up into!" Likewise, our commitment to our students does not end with their graduation!

Philip Zimbardo's message in his classic study, "The Lucifer Effect," is loud and clear: prisons under their current conditions are intrinsically inhumane places. Many would compare them to the boot training of soldiers. They also are deprived of many liberties. True, but . . . the military puts something noble back into the person. We publicly say, "Thank you for your service." No convict has ever heard the words, "Thank you for your service!"

Through creativity, Ewen Montagu produced the world's greatest act of deception. It is no secret what makes us good people: community service. We don't need a "fox" to monitor our daily activities. Racial profiling has created an imbalance in our jails and prisons. We need to look no further than the UNESCO REPORT for scientific proof of the equality of everyone. The potential of the teaching profession is beyond limit. Everyone in America sits at our feet for many years.

At Shawnee Mission Northwest we taught with the mission statement that "Students Are Number One." Schools do not exist primarily for teacher employment. Our final product is nothing short of the future.

Those that can, teach! Those who cannot are in some other profession!

Chapter 16

From Russia with Questions

Keep on sowing your seed, you never know which will grow—perhaps
it all will!

—Paraphrase of Ecclesiastes 11:6

Would the community service class be an effective adjunct to the Russian
educational system? This chapter documents an effort to transplant the
CCC into the heart of Russia.

To escape making this either a travelogue or a diary, let's highlight how
the Russian teachers considered something new to their educational system.
With the collapse of communism in the 1990s, efforts were made by both the
Russians and the United States to mutually share their various methods. Russia's system has resulted in their country reaching 98 percent literacy! Even
under Stalin, education has always been a national priority.

Forty Russians teachers visited the United States to both understand our
system and garnish some potential new ideas. They were representing the
best of their system. Their English was perfect. Since the fall of the communist system, Russia had been divided into numerous independent countries.
Each Russian teacher was eager to have an American teacher to visit and to
share ideas. In effect, this was a new experience for them as well as us.

Fifteen progressive US teachers were chosen to represent our various
programs of education. Hopefully, each of us represented something that
would be of value to our Russian visitors. EAST and WEST initially met at
the University of Delaware for several days. This would give them some idea
of some aspect of the American system that could be of use to them. After
brief presentations, Russians could express their preferences on what teacher/
program would be of benefit to them.

How did community service fare with the forty experts? This constituted a challenge to represent the United States and my students as well. The respect was nothing short of electric! Some were actually in tears! This program was exactly what they wanted for their changing system. It is no exaggeration to say that promises of "gifts" were offered for the sponsor to choose their city. "We will daily serve you orange juice (a luxury)," "We will take you to opera or the symphony," "We will keep you warm (Siberia)." It was a relief to know that many of the CCC achievements were well represented and well received.

A sort of "Deus ex Machina" made the decision for everyone. The sponsor was going to Togliatti, Gymnasium #9. Dinara Zakhorove would be a Russian host. Togliatti was a day's train trip from Moscow. The destination was at last fixed and about to commence. Then suddenly a strange feeling arose within the sponsor. Emotional baggage!

As an elementary student in a small city in the Midwest, the threat of a communist invasion quickly was ever present. Air raid practices involved quickly sitting under our desk, hands over our heads, waiting for the all clear voice. Nikita Khrushchev's famous threat, "We will bury you" was not taken as an idle matter. Our entire city had to be in darkness as an air raid was expected.

One family had been arrested because they left a yard light on! Even church services ended with prayers for the conversion of Russia. Now the sponsor would be the guest of the very country which had in effect robbed me of a peaceful childhood. To make matters even worse, one of the fathers of an American teacher all but disowned her for even agreeing to go to Russia. Latent feelings were actually at the top of visiting what Reagan called "the evil empire."

In a graphic attempt to rid his country of anything religious, Stalin had dynamited the largest Russian orthodox church in the world, The Cathedral of Christ the Savior. Before destroying the inscribable edifice, he removed any religious objects of value. In its place he constructed a swimming pool for the summer and a skating rink for the winter! To see the actual incident, key in *The Cathedral of Christ the Savior* for its actual demolition in 1931.

As the American was about to enter his first Russian classroom, the department chairperson admonished him "not to mention God unless the students do." That which is forbidden is attractive! After the students sat down, the sponsor's first words a thanksgiving to God for making this visit possible! The students were alive with genuine interest in the CCC. Their English was nearly perfect. For nearly an hour they learned and accepted the basic concept, *The Doer of Good becomes Good.* As a result, they began to think of ways to implement that mission statement. Then something strange—very strange—happened.

At the sound of the bell, each student individually expressed their gratitude to the American. Young Sergei was hesitant to leave. He asked if he could return for the next hour. "If you can get out, you can come in!" He returned and sat directly in front of the teacher. He appeared to be in a daze. At the conclusion of the class, he said, "Ronald, this is the greatest thing I have ever learned." He received a crushing hug in gratitude.

It was obvious he wanted to say more. He appeared a bit awkward. He had believed all the anti-American propaganda. His covert religious faith had been stifled for years. He lowered his head, clutching an American pencil, a picture of the Kansas Capital, a handful of pennies, he said something no one else heard, "God bless you Ronald, and all of America." Sergei was the only Russian during the entire visit that invoked God's blessing. It remains a very special memory.

The entire experience was exhausting. High schools, universities, even a radio broadcast. On one occasion, the sponsor actually fell asleep during a presentation by a panel of Russian students! What became very obvious was the ordinary Russian had nothing but admiration for the United States. After many presentations, it was not uncommon for large groups—both students and teachers—asking for the American sponsor to find some way to get these young Russians out of the country. They wanted an American of any age for marriage. They had given up and were unwilling to give their new government a try.

The overwhelming positive reception of the CCC's philosophy was far from anticipated. The object was simply to share. The Russian Minister of Education published a synopsis of the community service class in the education journal, *The Active School*. With twenty-six years of community service, it is fair to say that only miracles will result in "the evil empire!" Student accolades could more than fill this entire book. Russia is in the process of changing.

Using the McClelland study as a guide, the value most embedded in the Russian textbooks, is the "achievement motive." Consequently, it has become the sixth choice of the world's foreign exchange students. Property collectivized by communism is in the process of being returned to private ownership. The educational system is changing and hopefully for the better. History is being rewritten; religious sentiment has become once again more overt. Let us use what might appear to be an extreme: JOSEPH STALIN.

Stalin remains one of the world's greatest murderers—even greater than Adolf Hitler. Like Alex, in *Clockwork Orange*, he had a fondness for violence (evil) and Mozart's Piano Concerto #23. One evening in 1944, it was performed by Maria Yadira on the radio. It brought the dictator to tears. Not knowing it was a live broadcast, he called the station and requested a recording to be delivered personally to him the next day at the Kremlin.

Fearing for their lives, the station assembled an orchestra and awoke Maria Yadira in the middle of the night.

Eventually three conductors led the orchestra. The record was pressed early in the morning. Fortunately, Stalin was unable to discern any differences. Let's process this.

Shades of Plato's universal soul theory of knowledge—according to Plato, we possess all knowledge within us. Only when we meet a proper stimulus, is that knowledge released. For Stalin, it was Mozart. He sent Maria Yadira 20,000 Rubles as a gift. She responded in a famous letter that said she would pray for his many sins. As for money, she had donated it to her church. A death notice was prepared but never signed. When Stalin died in 1953, that recording was spinning on his record player. The last sounds he heard on earth was Mozart.

You can actually hear that piano concerto online and see the actual record hand-made for Stalin. Look it up, it may touch you in a similar manner.

In a similar manner, is it far-fetched to believe that community service could change the average Russian student? Are Russian students any different than American students? The Doer of Good becomes Good in any country. Any number of megatons will never equal one good deed! The CCC mustard seed has been planted. We can only hope that it will grow and blossom in what we used to call "the evil empire!"

Returning to Shawnee Mission Northwest was an emotional reunion for all. The CCC class had functioned completely on its own. They had completed several original projects. The class president had simply taken over. A student traveled 110 miles away to receive an award to the sponsor! Not one student was truant. A reception at the district administration office, complete with refreshments was a touching tribute for a life-changing and enhancing program. One month later, the sponsor received a letter from a Russian woman. She had given me her Lenin Young Pioneer pin. The letter simply said: "Ronald, we are sorry for what we have done to the world."

After this experience, and as I end my teaching career, I feel like David in the Old Testament. All he had was a single stone. I have but one rock, The CCC, may it be the source of change we all want. In the words of Isaiah:

> "And they shall beat their swords into plowshares and their spears into pruning hoods; nations shall not lift up sword against nations, neither shall they learn war anymore."

Appendix A

Community Comments

Dear members of the CCC: You are truly wonderful, caring and impressive people! Thank you for your very generous donation. We realize that this grand check means many hours of hard work and a "dollar day" at school. Please know that we appreciate the opportunity to be able help our patients. Do not underestimate the importance of your gift.

Volunteer Services Department, Visiting Nurse Association

Simply put, I was blown away by your willingness to help and to be touched by your goodness. Thank you for your dream of Cougars Community Commitment!

Community Resident

On behalf of the board and staff of Associated Youth Services, THANK YOU. None of our services would be possible without involved and committed people like you, the CCC.

Director: Associated Youth Services

Thank you for making health kits to give to needy families. Without the help of the CCC, we would not have been able to provide so many families with necessary hygiene items.

St. Luke's Lutheran Church

Thanks to the CCC program at SMNW High School for providing a student fourth period as a peer for Jessica, a disabled student in a wheelchair. You have no idea (the) joy Ashley brought to Jessica's life. I cannot say enough good things about this program.

Special Education Department, SMNW High School.

CCC teaches one of the most valuable lessons life has to offer, that (of) being of service to fellow human beings, and getting that feeling of satisfaction that only comes from selfless giving.

"Job Olympics"

There are few, if any, higher-level classes that I had found before this year that taught anything as life-changing as CCC. The lessons of compassion, philanthropy, and the basic quality of all humanity regardless of age, faith, or socioeconomic status come from experiences that the students volunteer themselves for, not a lecture or book. CCC opens the heart as well as the mind!

National Merit Scholar, SMNW High School

This was the only class I looked forward to during my four years at NW. Honestly, it changed my whole life!

Anonymous senior

Awards

No person was ever honored for what he received. Honor has been the reward for what he gave.

—Calvin Coolidge

Public recognition is evidence of the intrinsic value and quality of the students' performances of the CCC. None of these awards was sought after but freely bestowed for their efforts on behalf of others. They range from local, state, national, and even international accolades. Numerous students received individual scholarship as a reward for their service. One student received a monetary award for 125,000 dollars: full college tuition! These awards are not the result of grades or any other academic achievements. Simply put, they are for what the service they have performed for others.

PENNEY'S GOLDEN RULE AWARD

Awarded the first year of its existence as a class. In the ensuing years, four individual students won awards from Penney's. One judge remarked to the sponsor, "We just assumed you would have someone in the running each year."

THE KANSAS CITY STAR

The *STAR* embarked on a journalistic feat that won local, state, and national awards. They chose twelve area programs that represented twelve different virtues essential to young people. The CCC was chosen to represent compassion. A reporter was assigned to the CCC for an entire semester. In effect, she enrolled in the class and attended many of our functions. The STAR devoted four pages of its Sunday paper to the CCC.

HABITAT II AWARD

A representative from Kansas University prepared a summary of the CCC for an international conference on volunteerism in Istanbul, Turkey.

SPIRIT OF GIVING AWARD

Kansas Governor, Bill Graves, presented his highest award to the CCC. The award was presented to the class at the State Capitol's Rotunda. The music for this event was provided by the Kansas State Prison Choir.

MISCELLANEOUS AWARDS

Individual service organizations presented their annual awards to the CCC. They included

1. Kaufman Foundation, School of Service Award: three years.
2. Optimists Club
3. Kiwanis Club
4. Sertoma Club
5. LaSertoma Club
6. Knights of Columbus
7. Lions Club
8. Newcomer's Spirit of Giving
9. Cards For Kansas City
10. City of Shawnee: CCC Day Celebration
11. Numerous individual students received scholarships based on their community service. In the long run, the real awards are the number of lives, both young and old, that are changed by the efforts of the students. Years later when returning students drop by for a visit, they mention that "the doer of good" is still part of their lives.

Appendix C

Tests and Methods

OBSERVATIONS TEST

This test is designed to establish how observant students are. Additional questions can be added to make this more pertinent for your group.

1. What is imprinted on the back side of the Jefferson nickel? (Monticello)
2. The portrait of which president is on the $20.00 bill? (Jackson)
3. How many red stripes are there in the American flag? (Seven)
4. One of the kings in a standard deck of cards is one eyed. Who? (Diamonds)
5. How many cards in a standard deck of cards including the jokers? (54)
6. How many dimes are there in a roll of dimes? (50)
7. How many keys on a standard piano? (88) 52 white, 36 black)
8. A snowflake has how many points? (6)
9. Which side are the buttons sewn on a man's shirt or jacket? (Right)
10. How many sides are on the familiar stop sign? (Eight)
11. On the computer keyboard over which number is the dollar sign? (Four)
12. A dial, rotary phone has how many holes? (Ten) (Push button: twelve)
13. Which letters are NOT included on the telephone dial? (Q and Z)
14. Which is the top color of a traffic light? (Red)
15. What is the name of the school principal?
16. What is the name of the current U.S. Vice President?
17. What color or colors are the student school lockers?
18. How many eyelets in your right shoe for shoe laces? Do not peek)
19. Are any of the school office walls painted a particular color
20. How many senators represent your state in Washington? Name on

HIDDEN ASSUMPTIONS TEST

The following test is designed to reveal hidden assumptions which prevent the solution of rather simple problems. The correct answers are on another page. Good luck!

Directions to the student: On your own paper answer the following questions. If you do not know the answer to the questions, immediate move to the next question. Please do not look at your neighbor's paper or ask for assistance.

1. Two men played chess. They played five games. Each man won three. Explain this.
2. Answer this question within five seconds and do not return to check your answer. How many animals of each species did Adam take aboard the Ark with him? Note: the question is not how many pairs, but how many animals.
3. An archaeologist reported that he had discovered two gold coins in the desert near Jerusalem dated 439 B.C. Why did his fellow scientists refuse to take his claim seriously?
4. If you had only one match and you entered a room to start a kerosene lamp, an oil heater, and a wood burning - stove, which would you light first and why?
5. Here is a question on international law: if an international airliner crashed exactly on the U.S. and Mexican border, where would you be required by law to bury the survivors?
6. You have four nines (9.9.9.9.) Arrange them to total 100. You may use any of the arithmetical processes (addition, subtraction, multiplication, or division. Each nine must be used once and only once.
7. Explain the following TRUE boast: "In my bedroom, the nearest lamp that I usually keep turned on is twelve feet away from my bed. Alone in the room, without using wires, strings or any other aids or contraptions, I can turn out the light on that lamp and get into the bed BEFORE the room is dark." Explain this.
8. Memorize the phrases below: As soon as you do that turn the paper over and write over and write them on your own paper from memory. Do not look back at the phrases once you have turned this page over.

Paris	Once	Bird		Slow
In the	In A	In the	Men At	
The Spring	A Lifetime.	The hand	At Work	

9. Explain why this is a very imprecise advertisement: "Four out of five doctors recommend Anacin."

FAKE ATTACK ANNOUNCEMENT

As an original student study, this fake attack on the United States was read by the vice-principal over the school's PA system but only to one freshman room and one senior room. Only the classroom teacher knew it was not real.

"Could I have your attention for an important all school announcement? Teachers please direct your students to give their complete attention to this announcement. We have just received word that Iran has attacked our fleet in the Persian Gulf and we have taken military action against them. State law requires that we inform you of this because the Ayatollah Khomeini has ordered Iranian terrorists in the US to attack specified targets. Several schools have already been attacked in various parts of the US. We are activating our civil defense procedures here at Northwest and I will give you further instruction as we hear from state authorities.

Teachers: please do not release any of your students until further notice from the office. Students: we need your total cooperation in this matter. At this time we would ask all teachers to review the civil defense procedures with their students. I will relay more information as it becomes available."

FRESHMAN CLASSROOM

Senior Classroom

Approximately two minutes later, a student entered the room and conveyed this was an experiment. Each student filled out a response questionnaire. The two classes responded completely opposite. Freshman: bomb 'em out, kill them, all of them.
Seniors: somber, quiet, afraid, worried about their future.

CIRCUMSTANCES TEST

During the first week of orientation, community service students take this quiz. Student answers are kept confidential. If possible, have the students answers these on a Scantron with either a fake name or emblem on it so they can retrieve their forms. This test will give you a "goodness quotient" for your class.

1. You buy something at a store. You receive more change back than you are entitled to. Would you (a) Keep it and leave or (b) give it back to the salesperson.

2. A friend of yours works in a store you frequent. He offers to "give" you some expensive merchandise free. You would a accept it, or(b) refuse he merchandise politely.

3. You move into an apartment or house. Cable TV was not disconnected. The service was not cancelled but never "cut off." Would you (a) keep it and say nothing or (b) tell the service company.

4. You are about to trade in your car for a new model. There is something seriously wrong with your car but the mechanic does not detect it. It makes your car worth much less if you tell the mechanic. You would (a) say nothing (b) tell the mechanic.

5. A friend of yours offers you some stolen merchandise at a very low price: worth $500 but your cost would be only $50. It is something you want. You would (a) buy it or (b) refuse it.

6. You are selling your home. Your basement has a serious water leak when it rains. This will cause potential buyers to pass up buying your home or reduce its value substantially. You would inform the buyer of this problem? (a) Yes (No).

7. A friend takes an exam early in the morning. You have that same class later in the day. He offers you correct answers to that exam which you will take later today. (a) refuse the answers, or (b) get as many as possible.

8. You find a wallet or purse with over $200 in it. Would you contact the owner and return the wallet/purse with all the money or would you say you found it without the money in it? You would (a) return it with the money or (b) return it without the money.

9. You work in a fast food place or theatre. Would you give extra or free food to your friend or admit them free to the movie? You would (a) Yes: free food or admittance; (b) No.

10. Income tax time: you itemize your deductions. You have a 99% chance of not being audited. You would or would not cheat to get a generous refund? (a) Yes (b) No.

11. You sell your automobile. The buyer asks you to state on the bill of sale a much lower sales price so his sales tax will be less. You would (a) refuse (b) lie and list a lower price.

12. You have high blood pressure or some other disease. You apply for life insurance. You are asked to report any diseases. The truth will result in not getting the policy or perhaps at a much higher cost. You would (a) lie or (b) tell the truth.

13. You take your family to a restaurant for a meal. Children under 12 are half price. Two of your three children are 14 and 15 but look much younger than their age. You would (a) order all adult meals or (b) lie about your two children's ages.

14. Your child asks you to write a fake note to school so he/she has an excused absence. Your fake note will save your child some serious consequences that will result from deliberate truancy. Would you (a) write a fake note or (b) not write a note and let your child take the consequences for truancy.

15. You attend an out-of-state school. Tuition for nonresidents is 300% higher. A friend offers you a local address so you will pay less. You would (a) accept the offer (b) refuse and pay more.

16. You order something from Sears. You break it when you opened it at home. Would you return it and say it arrived broken. You would (a) lie about it or (b) pay for a repair.

17. You are offered a good job that requires you to work late hours on school nights. Your grades will be greatly affected. Pay is $15.00 an hour. You would (a) accept or (b) reuse the job offer.

18. You buy a CD and do not like it. Would you return it and say it was defective or simply keep it because the policy is no returns except for defective items. You would (a) keep it (b) return it and lie.

19. You apply for life insurance. The agent asks you if you smoke so he can offer you a lower premium. You smoke. Would you (a) lie and get a lower rate or (b) tell the truth and pay more.

20. Your best friend asks you to lie so he/she will either not go to jail or will not have to pay a large fine. You would (a) lie (b) tell the truth.

THE DIFFERENT METHODS TO USE
FOR ORIGINAL STUDIES

Listed below are the various "types" of studies you can employ in your original studies. Although the techniques vary, the end result is still the same: analysis of human activity.

1. Cross Sectional Study
   A study which limits its observations to a single point in time. E.G. Campbell (1959) interviewed a national same of 1,713 young women to discover their childbearing frequency and expectations.

2. Longitudinal Study
   If the study extends over time, describing a trend or making a before and after set of observations, it is called longitudinal. E.G., does the authoritarianism of the military carry over when a cadet leaves the military?

3. Ex-post Facto Study

    This study seeks to trace a present situation back to some earlier factors which may have been involved. What you are going to study has already happened. You dig into the past to find out the reason.

4. Planned Study

    The concept involved here is very simple yet affective: hold all variables constant except one: cause it to vary and see what happens. E.G. give a vitamin to one group and a placebo to another control group. Check and compare the results.

5. Observation Study

    Observational studies are like planned experiments in respects except one: in the planned experiments the scientist arranges for something to happen so that he can observe what follows, whereas in the observational study the scientist observes something happen by itself—he does not cause anything to happen. E.G. What kind of cars are in the Northwest parking lot?

6. Impressionistic study

    This is the study you do when you cannot do anything thing else. E.G. A tour of Russia with no opportunity for controlled scientific investigation.

7. Statistical Comparative Study

    Much research consists of looking up recorded statistical facts and comparing and interpreting them. E.G. Are more women today than fifty years ago remaining single?

8. Questionnaire Study

    The facts are not recorded anywhere. You can find them by only asking people. E.G. What is the ideal family size today? They are more reliable than simple guesswork.

9. Participant Study

    Taking an active part to seek insights by participation in the study. E.G. John Howard Griffin in 1961 passed as a Black person to understand racism in America. These studies are delightful and fun to do.

10. Case Study

    A complete, detailed account of some phenomenon. E.G. What is it like to obtain a divorce? To be a drop out from school? To be a run away? Live in a nursing home?

Appendix D

Forms

We live, unfortunately, in a society inundated with legalities. For twenty-six years, these forms have served us well and cover almost any eventuality. In most cases, permissions require three signatures: the student, sponsor, and the parents. To date, there have been no legal difficulties due to the use of these forms.

Disclaimer: please allow your building administration and district legal personnel to approve appropriate forms for your needs. You may copy any material from these forms that is necessary. The focus in this book is not intended for individual school or district use. They are merely what has worked for the CCC and are intended to be a guide/example.

CCC INTRODUCTION FORM

Name_____ Junior _____ Senior

Address_____ Phone _____ Cell _____

1. What kind of car to you have? _____

2. Do you have a truck or access to one? _____

3. Please list your hobbies _____

4. Do you have a job? _____

5.   If so, where do you work?_____
      Hours a week?_____

6.   Weekends: are you available for projects on weekends, especially
      Saturdays?_____

7.   Do you have a special interest: cars, movies, music, etc. _____
      _____

8.   Based on your interests, other students' comments, etc. what kind
      of service are you especially interest in?

      ____Tutoring _____ Lawn care _____ Elderly _____
      Community Center _____ Animals

9.   How do you rate yourself as a conversationalist with adults?
      _____

10.   Do you like to do any of the following:

      _____ fish _____ dance _____ sing _____ play pool
      _____ play cards _____Crafts

11.   Would you like to tutor in math or computers to elementary
      students? ____Yes _____No

12.   Are you willing to car pool and/or take someone (another student)
      in your car if needed?
      Emergencies_____

13.   Can you bring any of the following:
      _____ Food _____ Clothing _____ money

14.   Do you have any special interests, e.g. cancer victims, disabilities,
      MS., etc. _____

15.   Why did you take this class?_____
      _____
      _____

Daily Schedule

Hour	Teacher	Room Number
1.	_____	_____
2.	_____	_____
3.	_____	_____
4.	_____	_____
5.	_____	_____
6.	_____	_____
7.	_____	_____

Lunch Period _____

Seminar Room _____

Any addition Comments:

_____

_____

_____

THE DOER OF GOOD BECOMES GOOD!

Assumption Test Answers

1. The men did not play each other. The assumption was they did.

2. Adam did not aboard the Ark. Noah did.

3. No one would know when Christ was coming. "B.C." assumes they did.

4. Easy: The match.

5. You do not bury survivors.

6. 99+9/9==100

7. The person does it in the daytime. Assumption: it was night.

8. There is an addition "the" "A" "the" "at" "Four out of Five Doctors recommend Anacin:" There are serval kinds of doctors including PhD's, ED, etc. The assumption, based on the product, was a medical doctor.

   Many statements are based on assumptions, e.g. a summer cold does not differ from any other cold; the higher the price, the better quality; as seen on TV, so what???

CCC CONTRACT

NAME_____HOUR_____

Cougars Community Commitment offers both YOU, the student, and the members of the local community a meaningful experience in LIFE. TRUST AND CARING are the key factors in making this class successful. As a member of this class, YOU agree to abide by the following:

1. To go to your daily commitment as quickly as possible. Always arrange transportation in advance of your activity.

2. To give genuine, caring service to each person in need, i.e., to apply your best effort continually.

3. You are permitted only five (5) absences. After five you must make them up.

4. GRADES are determined by attendance and the number of hours of community service given each QUARTER. Your performance may also be critiqued by whomever is in charge of the site you visit.

5. ALWAYS inform your site in advance if you are not going to be there. This is very important and can affect your grade!

6. ONE TRUANCY WILL RESULT IN THE STUDENT BEING DROPPED FROM THIS CLASS. THIS IS ABSOLUTE AND HAS NO LIMITATIONS. EVEN IF THE TRUANCY OCCURS DURING THE FINAL DAYS OF THE QUARTER OR SEMESTER, THE STUDENT WILL BE DROPPED WITH LOSS OF ALL CREDIT.

7. If a misunderstanding occurs between the student and the person/place he/
she is giving service, the matter will be resolved by a meeting with the
person, student and class sponsor.

There are many scholarships and awards based on community service. Your
input, questions, and suggestions are always welcomed. Remember one
simple mission statement:

THE DOER OF GOOD BECOMES GOOD!!

_____	_____
Student Signature	Parent/Guardian Signature

_____	_____
Sponsor	Date

CCC   Name_____

Hour _____

OFF CAMPUS PARENTAL PERMISSION FORM

The Shawnee Mission School District offers a number of courses and activities which have both classroom, instruction and community work experience,
observations, and performances. Courses which require community based
experiences are Biology 2H, Consortium, Exploring Childhood I and II,
Fashion Careers II, Health Careers, Advanced Journalism, Marketing Education II, Business Technology II, Radio & TV Production, ROTC, Sociology
II, U.S. History AP, Yearbook, International Languages, classes taught at
other Shawnee Mission schools, community college classes, Cougars Community Commitment, PACE courses, some special education and vocational
classes.

REQUEST FOR SPECIAL ENROLLMENT

Name _____

Student #_____

I/we, the parents, of the above named student, request that he/she be permitted to participate in these courses and/or activities for the 2012-2013 school year. I/We have read the course information provided by the school at the time of enrollment and agree to the conditions for participation. I/We understand that the Shawnee Mission School District does not provide transportation for enrolled students and that no insurance of any sort is provided for students participating in courses with community work experience, observation, or performance activities. For those students going to vocational training classes off the Northwest campus where the district provides bussing, it is strongly recommended that the student ride the bus to their location. If they choose not to ride the bus, the school will not provide transportation or insurance to participate in this program. My/Our signatures below indicate that I/We understand and approve the enrollment and participation of our student in the above named course and are willing to assume the responsibilities and risks in participation. NOTE: This is not an open lunch permit.

Parent Signature_____ Date _____

_____

Dear Parent/Guardian:

You probably already signed a code six form when your child enrolled at Northwest. I want you to know what this form means to my C.C.C. class.

1. Your child will drive his/her car every day to his/her community service location.
2. Your child may car pool with another student and can ride in a car driven by another student.
3. Any accident is covered by your child's personal insurance.
4. It is my expectation that all of my students will observe all driving and traffic regulations.

If you have any questions, please feel free to contact me at 913-993-7359.

Ronald W. Poplau, Sponsor, Cougars Community Commitment.

GRADES

Grades are important. These indicate how well you are doing in any subject as well as in CCC. I cannot stress enough how important it is to have community service on your school transcript. You are free to come anytime to note your class progress and to insure that I have given you credit for all that you do. At least twice during each quarter you will get an hour's report plus the district's progress report.

1. You may have only five (5) excused absences per quarter. After five you are expected to make them up. You are not permitted to make up an unexcused absence. Any activity you do on a code six form does not count against you or from the school. You must give me the code six form before you leave on the activity, e.g. Turn Styles.

2. Each activity you do will have an "hour" value. E.G. spending the day at Turn Styles Thrift Store is six hours of service, 9:00 a.m. to 2:30 p.m. A dozen home-made cookies is an hour of credit. When in doubt ASK!

3. Grades are as follows:

Per Quarter
1. 18–20 hours above the class is an A
2. 16–17 Hours is a B
3. 14–15 Hours is a C
4. 12–13 Hours is a C
Hours overlap into the next quarter. e.g. if you earn six the first quarter and then 30 the next, you will receive a final grade of A.

Per Semester
1. 36–40 Hours above the class is an A
2. 32–35 Hours is a B
3. 28–31 Hours is a C
4. 24–27 Hours is a D
All outside hours need to be approved in advance. You may NOT just hand me a list of things that you have done. Please note this well to avoid and disappointments later. No attempt will be made to help you gain hours if you have ignored all other possibilities. Don't wait until the last moment.

THE DOER OF GOOD BECOMES GOOD!

A Grading Option

Many of you have other time constraints which limit your availability for extensive participation in CCC Activities: Sports; jobs; or other time consuming activities. You may wish to adopt the following grade option:

1. Attend your daily site with no negative evaluations.
2. Attendance requirements—not to exceed five excused absences.
3. This would give you a grade of C.
4. Everyone will be required to bring ten (10) cans of food PER QUARTER for a semester total of 20 cans.

Some Activities for Hours

1. Bring cookies for Cappuccino Day: an hour per dozen.
2. Pop Tabs for Ronald McDonald House: an hour per sandwich bag.
3. Turn Styles Thrift Store Volunteer: seven hour per day.
4. Thanksgiving Day Meal: With Turkey: 8 hours; w/o Turkey: 5 hours.
5. Child Care for PTA meetings.
6. Letter writing to Shawnee Gardens Nursing home: list of residents in 208.
7. Blood Donation: 3 hours.
8. Faculty Secret Pals.
9. Box Tops for Education.

   Individual Projects: see me first

CCC ATTENDANCE SHEET

NAME:_____ SITE: _____

Each day the CCC Student is required to sign in with you. Please put the form where the student will sign in/sign out each time they come to your room!

Date

1. _____In_____Out_____

2. _____In_____Out_____

3. _____In_____Out_____

4. _____In_____Out_____

5. _____In_____Out_____

6. _____In_____Out_____

7. _____In_____Out_____

8. _____In_____Out_____

9. _____In_____Out_____

10. _____In_____Out_____

11. _____In_____Out_____

12. _____In_____Out_____

13. _____In_____Out_____

14. _____In_____Out_____

15. _____In_____Out_____

16. _____In_____Out_____

17. _____In_____Out_____

18. _____In_____Out_____

19. _____In_____Out_____

Date

20. _____In_____Out_____

21. _____In_____Out_____

22. _____In_____Out_____

23. _____In_____Out_____

24. _____In_____Out_____

25. _____In_____Out_____

26. _____In_____Out_____

27. _____In_____Out_____

28. _____In_____Out_____

29. _____In_____Out_____

30. _____In_____Out_____

31. _____In_____Out_____

32. _____In_____Out_____

33. _____In_____Out_____

34. _____In_____Out_____

35. _____In_____Out_____

36. _____In_____Out_____

37. _____In_____Out_____

38. _____In_____Out_____

39. _____In_____Out_____

40. _____In_____Out_____

41. _____In_____Out_____

42. _____In_____Out_____

References

Brasch, Rudolph. 1965. *How Did It Begin?* New York: David McKay Company.
———. 1973. *How Did Sex Begin?* New York: David McKay Company.
———. 1976. *Strange Customs*. New York: David McKay Company.
Brown, Henry Floyd. 1998. *Real Prison, A Life in Poetry*, Hong Kong: Lotus Printing Press.
Carpenter, Edmund S. 1970. *They Became What They Beheld*. New York: E.P. Dutton.
French, Scott. 1993. *Just This Once*. New York: Carol Publishing Group.
Fried, SuEllen, and Paula Fried. 1996. *Bullies and Victims*. New York: M. Evans.
Frontline PBS. 2017. *Last Days of Solitary*. Season 35, Episode 13.
Gardner, Robert. 1963. *Dead Birds*. Documentary Education Films. Watertown, Main.
Glueck, Sheldon, and Glueck, Eleanor. 1952. *Delinquents in the Making*. New York: Harper and Row.
Howard, Ted, and Jeremy Rifkin. 1977. *Who Should Play God?* New York: Dell Publishing Company.
Hunt, Paul, and Chester Horton. 1964. *Sociology*, Second Edition. New York: McGraw Hill.
Iannucci, Armando. 2017. *The Death of Stalin*. Motion Picture.
James, Clifton. 1954. *I Was Monty's Double*. New York: McGraw Hill.
Johnson, L.D. 1970. *The Devil's Front Porch*. Kansas: University Press.
Kubrick, Stanley. 1971. *A Clockwork Orange*. Motion Picture.
McCelland, David. 1987. *The Achievement Motive*. New York: Appleton-Century-Crofts.
Montagu, Ewen. 1954. *The Man Who Never Was*. Philadelphia: Lippincott.
Perrault, Gilles. 1964. *The Secret of D-Day*. Boston: Little, Brown and Company.
Redesigning Man: Science and Human Values. Filmstrips, Marion McDaniel, and Michael McDaniel. 1974. New York: Harper and Row.

Rovin, Jeff. 2000. *Why Do Cowboys Wear High Heels?* American Media: Mini Mags. Inc.

Secunda, Victoria. 1984. *By Youth Possessed*. New York: Bobbs Merrill.

Silence of the Heart. 1984. DVD. Mariette Hartley, Actor; Charlie Sheen, Actor.

Sorokin, Pitirim A. 1964. *Basic Trends of Our Times*. New Haven, Conn: College Press.

Spitz, Rene. 1945. "Hospitalism." In *The Psychoanalytical Study of the Child*, Vol. 1 (pp. 53–74). New York: International Universities Press Inc.

UNESCO. 1951. *The Race Concept*. Paris: UNESCO Publications.

Yadira, Maria. ABC Classic 2. The Last Music Stalin Heard Was Mozart.

Zimbardo, Philip. 2007. *The Lucifer Effect*. New York: Random House Media.

About the Author

Ron Poplau was involved in community service and social science for 55+ years and has been a Coordinator of Continuing Education for several Universities. He is a member of the Kansas, Mid-America, and National Teacher's Halls of Fame, and was the 2006 Kansas Teacher of the Year and a finalist for National Teacher of the Year. He was a consultant to numerous school districts throughout the country and was a delegate of the State Department to Russian Schools exploring the benefits of community service to students.

Lightning Source UK Ltd.
Milton Keynes UK
UKHW042350180219
337566UK00001B/72/P

9 781475 848540